DATE DUE

FOLLETT

—African-American Biographies—

NIKKI GIOVANNI

Poet of the People

Series Consultant:
Dr. Russell L. Adams, Chairman
Department of Afro-American Studies, Howard University

Judith Pinkerton Josephson

Enslow Publishers, Inc.

40 Industrial Road	PO Box 38
Box 398	Aldershot
Berkeley Heights, NJ 07922	Hants GU12 6BP
USA	UK

http://www.enslow.com

To Nikki Giovanni, a weaver of words, whose cooperation and contributions were invaluable in writing this book.

Library of Congress Cataloging-in-Publication Data

Josephson, Judith Pinkerton.
  Nikki Giovanni, poet of the people / Judith Pinkerton Josephson.
    p. cm. — (African-American biographies)
  Includes bibliographical references and index.
  Summary: Profiles the life of Nikki Giovanni, from her childhood in Knoxville and Cincinnati to her career as an outspoken, influential, award-winning poet.
  ISBN 0-7660-1238-7
  1. Giovanni, Nikki—Juvenile literature. 2. Giovanni, Nikki—Political and social views—Juvenile literature. 3. Poets, American—20th century—Biography—Juvenile literature. 4. Afro-American women poets—Biography—Juvenile literature. [1. Giovanni, Nikki. 2. Poets, American. 3. Afro-Americans—Biography. 4. Women—Biography.] I. Title. II. Series.
PS3557.I55 Z74 2000
811'.54—dc21
                                                                    99-050864
Printed in the United States of America

10 9 8 7 6 5 4 3

Permission to quote excerpts and poems from the following, protected by copyright (© Nikki Giovanni), has been granted by Nikki Giovanni, author:
Selected Poems of Nikki Giovanni (William Morrow and Company, 1996); *Black Feeling, Black Talk/Black Judgement* (William Morrow and Company, 1970); *Re: Creation* (Broadside Press, 1970); *My House* (William Morrow and Company, 1972); *Ego-Tripping and Other Poems for Young People* (Lawrence Hill Books, 1973, 1993); *Cotton Candy on a Rainy Day* (Morrow Quill Paperbacks, 1980); *The Sun Is So Quiet* (Henry Holt and Company, 1996); *Those Who Ride the Night Winds* (William Morrow and Company, 1983); *Sacred Cows . . . and Other Edibles* (William Morrow and Company, 1988); *Grand Mothers: Poems, Reminiscences, and Short Stories About the Keepers of Our Traditions* (Henry Holt and Company, 1999); *Blues: For All the Changes* (William Morrow, 1999); *Love Poems* (William Morrow and Company, 1998); *Grand Fathers: Reminiscences, Poems, Recipes, and Photos of the Keepers of Our Traditions* (Henry Holt and Company, 1999).

To Our Readers: We have done our best to make sure all Internet addresses in this book were active and appropriate when we went to press. However, the author and the publisher have no control over and assume no liability for the material available on those Internet sites or on other Web sites they may link to. Any comments or suggestions can be sent by e-mail to comments@enslow.com or to the address on the back cover.

Illustration Credits:
© Barron Claiborne, by permission of Nikki Giovanni, p. 6; Bert Berinsky, courtesy of Nikki Giovanni, p. 60; Bob Veltri, Virginia Tech, pp. 82; Courtesy of Nikki Giovanni, pp. 47, 67, 75; Courtesy of Yolande Giovanni, pp. 17, 19, 25, 29, 32; By permission of *Ebony* Magazine, Johnson Publishing Company, p. 41; Fox Productions & the NAACP Image Awards, p. 9; Gary Agliata, p. 93; Karen Dolan, by permission of William Morrow and Company, Inc., p. 70, 109; Linda Dixon, p. 103; Mari Evans, by permission of Nikki Giovanni, p. 111; Marion Ettlinger, p. 98; Rick Griffiths, Virginia Tech, pp. 77, 84, 89, 99; Victoria Lucas, by permission of Nikki Giovanni, p. 52.

Cover Credit: Rick Griffiths, Virginia Tech

CONTENTS

Acknowledgments

For their time and valuable insight into Nikki Giovanni's life and work, thanks to Yolande Giovanni, Ann Ford, Linda Dixon, Gloria Haffer, Hamilton Cloud, Marquetta Cheeks, and the NAACP Image Awards, Doris Cooper, and Daryl Dance. For "For Nikki: Nommo," thanks to Margaret Bristow. For reading and editing the manuscript, thanks to Virginia Fowler, Edith Fine, Catherine Koemptgen, and Melissa Irick. As always, thanks to Donna, Marie, Karen, Kathleen, Jodie, Stephanie, and Suzan for listening as each chapter unfolded.

1

"BUT SINCE YOU FINALLY ASKED"

ressed in a sleek black pants suit, poet Nikki Giovanni stood alone onstage at the 1998 Image Awards in Pasadena, California. Against the glittering backdrop, Giovanni, five feet two, looked small. Her honey-brown face was dotted with freckles and framed by tightly cropped, white-blond hair. For the show's finale, she would recite part of her poem "But Since You Finally Asked," written in 1993 to honor African people brought to America as slaves.

Speaking in a strong, clear voice, but matter-of-fact tone, Giovanni began:

Nikki Giovanni

No one says . . . "What I like about your people" . . . then ticks off the wonder of the wonderful things . . . we've given . . . Our song to God, Our strength to the Earth . . . Our unfailing belief in forgiveness . . .

Softly, a clicking sound began to punctuate the poet's words. Behind her, dancer and Broadway star Savion Glover tap-danced lightly down a flight of stairs. (HEEL-AND-TOE, DOWN A STEP, HEEL-AND-TOE, DOWN A STEP, CLICK-A-CLICK-A, CLICK-A-CLICK-A, TAP, TAP, TAP.) Giovanni paused, listening.

At the base of the stairs, Glover's feet brushed the stage floor. (SCUFF-FLAP, SCUFF-FLAP, TAPPETA-TAP-TAP.) He moved forward.

I know what I like about us . . . is that we let no one turn us around . . . not then . . . not now . . . we plant our feet . . . on higher ground . . .

Glover leaped and planted *himself* on a raised wooden platform midstage. Faster and faster moved his shiny shoes. His tapping echoed her crisply spoken words. Heels and toes slapped the polished wood, some steps loud, other steps soft.

Giovanni nodded her head and smiled. Her body swayed gently to Glover's staccato beat.

I like who we were . . . and who we are . . . and since someone has asked . . .

Her hands swept the air. Glover's tapping became a steady drumming.

let me say: I am proud to be a Black American . . . I am proud that my people labored honestly . . . with forbearance and dignity . . . I am proud that we believe . . . as no other people do . . . that all are equal in His sight . . .

Giovanni stood quietly. With clenched fists, Glover punched the air. He whirled and twirled, his feet a blur, dreadlocked hair flying. The audience, stunned at first, clapped, whistled, and cheered loudly.

We didn't write a constitution . . . we live one . . . We didn't say "We the People" . . . we are one . . . We didn't have to add . . . as an after-thought . . . "Under God" . . . We turn our faces to the rising sun . . . knowing . . . a New Day . . . is always . . . beginning

Glover's tapping bounced like steel spikes against a tin wall. From the audience, more clapping, shouting, then silence. His footsteps slowed. The tapping softened to a gentle patter. Glover moved downstage to where Giovanni stood. He stopped and jumped forward. Then he playfully linked arms with her. To wild applause, the poet and the dancer strolled off the stage.

◆ ◆ ◆ ◆ ◆

Hamilton Cloud was the executive producer of the 1998 Image Awards, sponsored by the National Association for the Advancement of Colored People (NAACP). When he suggested that Giovanni and Glover perform together in the finale of the show, Cloud had a hunch the result would be magical. It was.

"I am proud to be a Black American": As Nikki Giovanni speaks the words of her poem, Broadway sensation Savion Glover tap-dances the beat.

Their performance was even more remarkable because until that night, Glover and Giovanni had not rehearsed together. Because of conflicts with schedules, each had rehearsed with a stand-in.

Cloud described that night's blending of these talents as "two jazz musicians riffing [improvising] off of each other." Of her, he said, "Nikki Giovanni is an icon. . . . She has a powerful presence as a person."[1]

Earlier in the star-studded ceremony, outstanding personalities in music, art, radio, television, film, literature, and other fields had received awards for their work. Giovanni had been particularly impressed with fellow award winner Kenneth ("Babyface") Edmonds's remarks about character. Edmonds quoted the words of Dr. Martin Luther King, Jr. The great civil rights leader had asked that people judge him and his people not by their skin color but by their character. Edmonds's remarks pointed to the history of African-American people. He said it left no doubt as to their character.

Nikki Giovanni's book *Love Poems* had won in the literature category. The award held special meaning for her. She and members of her family had long been active in the NAACP and other groups working for the civil rights of African Americans.

Giovanni's NAACP award is just one of many honors she has received in her career. She has published twenty-seven books and has received numerous awards, as well as fourteen honorary degrees from colleges and universities. She has been given the keys to more than a dozen cities, including New York City and Los Angeles.

As she did in her performance with Glover, Giovanni has often combined her poetry with music in albums, CDs, or live performances. Her poems mirror the rhythm, flow, and message of the gospel, blues, and jazz music she loves. Her words pay tribute to the energy of the young, the strength of the downtrodden, and the wisdom of the old.

Giovanni believes that poetry should tell the truth. She wants her poetry to connect her with ordinary people, almost as if she sat chatting with them on the front porch. Threaded through her poetry are Giovanni's strong beliefs about racism, sexism, the environment, and current events.

When writer Lorraine Dusky interviewed Giovanni in 1973, she wrote, "Nikki Giovanni glows with assurance and stamina and strength: black pride that could knock you over. Her voice has steel in it—ain't nobody gonna stop this lady. . . ." Yet Dusky also described Giovanni's warmth and openness: "She'd like to take everybody home to her heart where she could pass out love like teacakes."[2]

Almost thirty years after this was written, Giovanni's passion for life still holds. Like all poets, she studies people and chooses her words carefully. She weaves stories about little things—driving a car down country roads, eavesdropping on truckers on a CB radio, what makes two friends friends, mother love, kisses, and why boys are like snowflakes.

Her poems are clear and direct, with "everything in plain sight," just the way she likes it.[3] But the feelings behind the words come straight from Nikki Giovanni's heart.

□□

But Since You Finally Asked

*(A Poem Commemorating the 10th Anniversary of the
Slave Memorial at Mount Vernon)*

*No one asked us . . . what we thought of Jamestown . . . in
1619 . . . they didn't even say . . . "Welcome" . . . "You're
Home" . . . or even a pitiful . . . "I'm Sorry . . . But We Just
Can't Make It . . . Without You" . . . No . . . No one said a
word . . . They just snatched our drums . . . separated us by
language and gender . . . and put us on blocks . . . where our
beauty . . . like our dignity . . . was ignored*

*No one said a word . . . in 1776 . . . to us about Freedom . . .
The rebels wouldn't pretend . . . the British lied . . . We kept
to a space . . . where we owned our souls . . . since we understood . . . another century would pass . . . before we owned
our bodies . . . But we raised our voices . . . in a mighty cry
. . . to the Heavens above . . . for the strength to endure*

*No one says . . . "What I like about your people" . . . then
ticks off the wonder of the wonderful things . . . we've given
. . . Our song to God, Our strength to the Earth . . . Our unfailing belief in forgiveness . . . I know what I like about us
. . . is that we let no one turn us around . . . not then . . . not
now . . . we plant our feet . . . on higher ground . . . I like who
we were . . . and who we are . . . and since someone has asked
. . . let me say: I am proud to be a Black American . . . I am
proud that my people labored honestly . . . with forbearance
and dignity . . . I am proud that we believe . . . as no other
people do . . . that all are equal in His sight . . . We didn't
write a constitution . . . we live one . . . We didn't say "We
the people" . . . we are one . . . We didn't have to add . . . as
an after-thought . . . "Under God" . . . We turn our faces to
the rising sun . . . knowing . . . a New Day . . . is always . . .
beginning.*[4]

2

"NIKKI-ROSA"

n her mother's side of the family, Nikki's grandmother, Emma Louvenia Watson, called Louvenia, was born in 1890. At nineteen, she married John Brown Watson in Albany, Georgia. A quiet, gentle man, he was twenty years older than his spirited second wife. On January 5, 1919, Louvenia gave birth to a daughter, Yolande Cornelia, Nikki Giovanni's mother.

Soon afterward, the Watsons left Albany—in a hurry. Nikki's grandmother had argued with a white shopkeeper about some lengths of cloth. Arguing with a white person was a dangerous thing for an African American to do. In many southern towns, lynchings of black people were still common.

Under cover of darkness, the Watsons left Albany and headed north, hidden in the back of a wagon. They got as far as Knoxville, Tennessee, where they bought a home in a black neighborhood at 400 Mulvaney Street.

Over the next three years, the Watsons had two more daughters—Anna (later shortened to Ann and nicknamed "Anto" by her nieces and nephews) and Agnes. Nikki's grandfather supported his family by teaching Latin at the all-black Austin High School and by tutoring. The scholarly John Brown Watson was nicknamed "Book."

"If anyone encountered a sign or word they couldn't read, they would ask John Watson," said Nikki's aunt Ann Ford.[1] John and Louvenia Watson made sure that all three daughters went to college.

Nikki's mother, Yolande, was bright and pretty and loved reading, art, and playing tennis. At Knoxville College in the mid-1930s, she met Jones Giovanni, called "Gus." Yolande found herself drawn to this handsome, well-dressed man with the broad grin and the unusual last name. Gus Giovanni had been born in Alabama in 1914 but later moved north to Cincinnati with his mother and brother. With scholarships, part-time jobs, and the help of a mentor, Gus also attended Knoxville College.

After graduation, Gus and Yolande married. On September 2, 1940, they had a baby girl. They named her Gary Ann. A few years later, Yolande again became pregnant. Popular guidebooks for parents told them to prepare a child for a new brother or sister. Hoping for a boy, Yolande Giovanni told Gary she would soon have a baby brother. The whole family started calling the coming baby Nikki.[2] When Yolande gave birth to another girl on June 7, 1943, the Giovannis named her Yolande Cornelia Giovanni, Jr. Gary nicknamed her new sister "Nikki-Rosa." As she grew, people shortened the name to "Nikki."

Even though both Yolande and Gus had earned college degrees, job choices for African Americans were limited. Gus worked as a bellhop in local hotels and stoked furnaces for a government agency. Shortly after Nikki was born, the Giovannis moved north to Cincinnati. There Gus and Yolande became house-parents at a home for African-American boys. Both of them enjoyed working with the boys, but the job still did not pay enough to support their family.

Then Gus Giovanni accepted a teaching position at South Woodlawn School. The family moved to Woodlawn, a northern suburb of Cincinnati. At that time in Ohio, and in many other states, black and white children went to separate schools. Woodlawn had no school for black children. So for second grade, Gary went to live with her aunt and uncle, Gladys and Bill Atkinson, in Columbus, Ohio. Bill was Gus Giovanni's half brother.

The Giovannis' Woodlawn house had no running

water. But Nikki did not mind. She even liked the outhouse. Besides, with Gary away, Nikki got to spend time with Mommy, all by herself. The house had a piano, which Nikki later said was a symbol of hope.[3] Her parents also filled their home with hundreds of books.

The next year the family moved to an apartment in nearby Wyoming, another Cincinnati suburb, where Gary could attend the all-black Oak Avenue School. Little Nikki liked the new neighborhood: "The sidewalks run broad and clear; the grass and mud intertwine just enough to let you be a muddy little lady; and there are those magnificent little violets that some called weeds and that I would pick for Mommy to put in her window vase."[4] Besides running and playing make-believe with the other kids, Nikki thought of herself as a champion swinger on swings.

When the time came for Nikki to start kindergarten in 1948, she would much rather have stayed home with her mother. She and Mommy read and did fun things together. That *had* to be better than school. To get Nikki ready for kindergarten, Gary taught her little sister letters, numbers, and a few dirty words.

Nikki adored her kindergarten teacher, Mrs. Scott, a warm, loving woman. Mrs. Scott taught the children school subjects, but also how to churn rich cream into butter. "I've never had butter that tasted that good," Giovanni recalled later.[5]

Dressed in her starched white Sunday dress, young

Nikki *looked* angelic. At least to adults. They saw her bright, smiling face sprinkled with freckles, her huge brown eyes, her hair tightly plaited into three pigtails, and her little white shoes, polished until they shone. Most of the time she obeyed her parents and her teachers. But the other children knew that Nikki was a scrappy spitfire.

Early in life, Nikki had decided her job was to protect her smart, beautiful, older sister, Gary. To Nikki, her sister was as regal and clever as a queen, just like

Nikki, front left, with the other first and second graders at Oak Avenue School in 1950.

Cleopatra and Nefertiti. *No one* would touch Gary, not if Nikki could help it.

Gary, three years older than Nikki, often stormed in from school or from piano lessons and announced to Nikki, "You've got to go fight Thelma [or Barbara or Flora] 'cause she's been messing with me."[6] This meant Gary had picked a fight with someone on the way home. Gary explained to Nikki that she *could* fight her enemies herself. But if she did, she might hurt her hands for the piano.

Nikki took her job as Gary's protector very seriously. Shortly after Nikki began kindergarten, she learned that a spindly, buck-toothed classmate of her sister's had been pulling Gary's hair and marking up her knees with a ballpoint pen. Nikki immediately challenged him to a marble duel.

Kids gathered around as Nikki drew a circle in the playground dirt. She shot marbles from between her legs. She tossed marbles over her back, and slipped in double spins. She not only beat the boy, but she also threatened to fight him if he did not leave her sister alone. Then Nikki strutted home, feeling smug. She hoped Mommy had made her favorite lunch of liverwurst with mayonnaise on raisin bread.

Nikki's sister came home from school as mad as a hornet. Gary told her mother that Nikki was picking on her friends. Nikki bolted out of the house, convinced it was all the boy's fault. She ran down the street, waving a broom and screaming his name. Soon the two were on the ground, arms and legs flailing. A crowd quickly gathered. Even in the thick of the fight, Nikki heard Mommy say, "I hope he gets her."[7]

Nikki's bravado popped like a balloon. The boy landed a square blow to Nikki's nose. Blood spurted out. Nikki did not cry, but stood glaring at her opponent. Meanwhile, Nikki's mother assured everyone that it was time Nikki stopped fighting Gary's battles. Nikki stomped home, feeling betrayed. But she had protected her beloved older sister.

By the time Nikki was in fourth grade, the family had moved to Lincoln Heights, a better, working-class

At an early age, Nikki, left, decided that her job in life was to protect her beloved older sister, Gary, right.

neighborhood. Her mother had started teaching third grade at St. Simon's, an all-black Episcopal school. Nikki went to school with her mother. Gary attended South Woodlawn School.

One of Nikki's favorite subjects at St. Simon's was writing. Students wrote stories, poetry, and letters. When the mother of one of the teachers died, the school's principal, Sister Winifred, had the children write sympathy letters. Nikki wrote:

Dear Miss Piersol,

I'm sorry your mother died. But it's just one of those things.

Sincerely,
Nikki Giovanni

Much to Nikki's embarrassment, Sister Winifred told the sensitive child, "We can't say *that*."[8]

Blessed with a quick mind and a feisty spirit, Nikki did well in school. Learning to read had opened a world brimming with new ideas and images. On days when she was sick and had to stay home, Nikki did not mind being by herself. She passed the time reading, writing, and doing math problems her father left for her.

Another good thing about St. Simon's was Sister Althea, Nikki's seventh-grade teacher. Most of the nuns who taught at the school were white. Sister Althea had been the first black nun accepted in the convent connected to the school. She became not only Nikki's teacher, but also her friend.

"Sister Althea was always encouraging . . . ," said Giovanni. "She thought I was smart. She was young at the time . . . so we kind of grew up together."[9]

The Giovanni family was poor, but Gus and Yolande stressed the importance of respect, love, education, and independence. From the gospel hymns her family sang at church, Nikki gained a strong sense of history and her own roots as an African American.

The Giovannis taught their girls to feel thankful for whatever they had. One Christmas, they both wanted bicycles. All Gus and Yolande could afford was roller skates. Yet Gus Giovanni thought of a way to make the girls feel less disappointed. When neighborhood children received bicycles for Christmas, Gus said, "Isn't it terrible that their parents gave them bicycles when it's so cold? They won't be able to ride until spring."[10]

One of Giovanni's most famous poems, "Nikki-Rosa," describes her childhood as one filled with love, family, happy times, and, always, hope. She has said of this poem: "I wanted to say, as the old gospel song so aptly expresses, 'It is well . . . with my soul.' I wanted to say that an outhouse, that a lack of some toys sometimes did not destroy my family. . . . for those of us whose fathers took them for Sunday rides in the better communities, that knowing there is more in life does not mean we were less. We had each other; and we had our dreams."[11]

Nikki-Rosa

childhood remembrances are always a drag
if you're Black
you always remember things like living in Woodlawn
with no inside toilet
and if you become famous or something
they never talk about how happy you were to have
your mother
all to yourself and
how good the water felt when you got your bath
from one of those
big tubs that folk in chicago barbecue in
and somehow when you talk about home
it never gets across how much you
understood their feelings
as the whole family attended meetings about Hollydale
and even though you remember
your biographers never understand
your father's pain as he sells his stock
and another dream goes
And though you're poor it isn't poverty that
concerns you
and though they fought a lot
it isn't your father's drinking that makes any difference
but only that everybody is together and you
and your sister have happy birthdays and very good
Christmases
and I really hope no white person ever has cause
to write about me
because they never understand
Black love is Black wealth and they'll
probably talk about my hard childhood
and never understand that
all the while I was quite happy[12]

3

"KNOXVILLE"

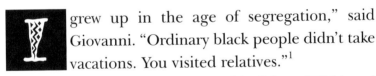

I grew up in the age of segregation," said Giovanni. "Ordinary black people didn't take vacations. You visited relatives."[1]

During summer vacations and holidays, Nikki and Gary spent time with their grandparents John and Louvenia Watson, in Knoxville, Tennessee. Aunts and uncles also visited, bringing Nikki's cousins—Haynes, Allison, William, and Terry.

The cozy family home at 400 Mulvaney Street was in a neighborhood where children bought flavored ices for a nickel. At night, "soft-voiced people" passed by the Watson home, saying, "Evening 'Fessor Watson, Miz Watson."[2]

On summer nights, Nikki and Gary huddled under the covers, giggling and singing. They read by the light of their Lone Ranger flashlight rings. Sometimes, they sneaked out of their room and huddled under the front window. There they eavesdropped on Grandmother and Grandpapa chatting on the front porch.

Nikki's grandmother was an activist, a real "stand-up person," as Giovanni later described her.[3] Grandmother Watson was honest, with a strong sense of right and wrong. She demanded obedience and "yes" answers from her grandchildren.

Aunt Ann, called "Anto," was often at Grandma Watson's house. She helped take care of Nikki, Gary, and their cousins.

"In those days, you had little white shoes," recalled Giovanni. "Anto would polish our shoes for going to church. . . . Then we would mess 'em up and she would want to kill us."[4]

Her niece's vivid imagination often impressed Anto. Nikki could make even a familiar story like "The Three Little Pigs" sound real. One summer night when Nikki was four or five, she could not sit still. She kept jumping up and running to the Watsons' front door.

"What are you doing, Nikki?" Anto asked.

"I want to go out and see if the wolf is there," said Nikki.

"What wolf?"

"The one that blew down the pigs' house. . . . I don't want him to huff and puff and blow *our* house down." Nikki looked for the wolf that whole summer.

Another day, when Anto asked Nikki what she wanted to do, she said, "Well, if you'll get me a salt-shaker, I'll catch me a bird." A popular saying was that if you sprinkled salt on a bird's tail, you could catch it.[5]

A family portrait. Front row, from left, the young cousins: William Chapman, Gary and Nikki Giovanni, Terry Chapman. Middle row: Ann ("Anto") Ford, Grandfather John Brown Watson, Grandmother Emma Louvenia Watson holding Haynes Ford, Jr., Yolande Giovanni (Nikki's mother), Agnes Chapman. Standing: Haynes Ford, Gus Giovanni (Nikki's father), William Chapman.

Summers in Knoxville were spent playing tennis at the playground across the street, sitting on the porch, and reading. Nikki loved the library, and she made friends with the librarian. During trips to places like Lookout Mountain, Nashville, or Chattanooga, Nikki and Gary played games in the car. They competed to see who could start the most nursery rhymes, such as "Henny Penny" and "Hickory, dickory, dock."

Both girls were disappointed when the movie *Snow White and the Seven Dwarfs* played at the whites-only theater. Nikki and Gary had to wait until it came to the black theater. Though Nikki was young, she also noticed that some Knoxville bathroom signs read "WHITE LADIES." Others read "COLORED WOMEN." In many public places at this time, the unfair separation of people by race, called segregation, was still legal.

No racial rules stopped people from listening to music on records or the radio. Nikki and Gary knew all the popular musicians—Tommy Dorsey, Duke Ellington, Louis Armstrong. When singer Billy Eckstine crooned, "What's My Name?" Grandmother Watson snapped, "Lord! Any fool know his name!"[6]

Playing the piano was something everyone in Grandma Watson's house tried. Though Nikki loved music, she balked at practicing scales on the piano.[7] Gary played much better than Nikki did.

Children often joined the adults at games. The card game canasta forced Nikki to count cards and learn her numbers. She became good enough at the word game Scrabble that she could almost beat Anto. Giovanni later wrote a poem about these lazy summer days in Knoxville:

Knoxville, Tennessee

I always like summer
best
you can eat fresh corn
from daddy's garden
and okra
and greens
and cabbage
and lots of
barbecue
and buttermilk
and homemade ice-cream
at the church picnic
and listen to
gospel music
outside
at the church
homecoming
and go to the mountains with
your grandmother
and go barefooted
and be warm
all the time
not only when you go to bed
and sleep[8]

When summers ended, Nikki and Gary went back to Cincinnati. In Nikki's later years at St. Simon's, her father took a job as a probation officer. He eventually found work for Yolande Giovanni, too. She quit her teaching job and became a social worker in the Hamilton County Welfare Department. With more money coming in, life for the Giovanni family became more comfortable.

Nikki graduated from eighth grade at St. Simon's in June 1957. In the fall, she started ninth grade at the black high school, Wayne High. Racial tensions were building in Cincinnati, just as they were across the country. In the famous 1954 court case *Brown* v. *the Board of Education of Topeka, Kansas,* the United States Supreme Court had ruled that students in all schools must be racially mixed, or integrated. This decision had caused ugly protests and clashes between whites and blacks.

A new Cincinnati high school, Princeton High, was almost finished. According to the Supreme Court, students of all races, including Nikki Giovanni, could attend. "Nobody knew how integration would work at Princeton High School," recalled Giovanni.[9]

After a year at Wayne High, Nikki called Grandmother Watson in Knoxville. She asked if she could spend the summer with her and Grandpapa, as usual. This time, she added, she wanted to stay on in Knoxville and attend Austin High in the fall. Grandmother Watson said yes.

"I wanted to live with Grandmother," said Giovanni. "But I also thought I would get better schooling there, too, even though Austin High School was still segregated."[10]

Living in Knoxville strengthened the special bond Nikki shared with her grandmother. Grandmother Watson provided warm comfort with actions as simple as braiding Nikki's hair. "Grandmothers put quilts over us and let us curl upon the couch and rock ourselves to sleep," Nikki has said.[11]

Both Nikki and her grandmother were opinionated, stubborn, and organized. But they got along well. "We both liked the house to smell and look the same way," said Nikki.[12] Louvenia Watson filled her kitchen with the aromas of feather-light rolls and homemade bread, peach or blackberry cobbler, and sherry chicken that fell off the bone.

Living with her grandparents also meant hard work and chores. One of Nikki's chores was waxing the floor.

Nikki and Grandmother Watson, right, shared a special bond.

"Grandma had a beautiful pantry. I would wax it so it would smell good. . . . I'd get that wax on the floor," said Giovanni, "and she would make rolls, biscuits, or corn bread. . . . We were a good team."[13]

Nikki and her grandmother also agreed about how the refrigerator should look. Nikki organized the food so it could be seen. She arranged the eggs in her grandmother's egg basket and lined up clear jars and bottles filled with juices and other foods.

Grandmother Watson was up at six o'clock, perking coffee and cooking grits. Monday was laundry day. "The trick to the washing," said Nikki, "was to put your sheets out the night before and sleep on the mattress cover. Otherwise, at the crack of dawn . . . she would snatch the sheets from under you, not only inconveniencing you but shaming you as well. . . . You were positively slovenly if you slept past six."[14]

Grandmother Watson had her quirks, too. Nikki knew that when Grandmother took a bath, she never remembered her soap. After she sank down into the steaming hot water, Nikki had to fetch the big, oval bar of pink, sweet-smelling Sweetheart soap.

Now that Louvenia Watson's daughters were grown, she had thrown herself into community activities—book club, bridge club, Bible school, garden club, playing piano for the Baptist young people, the black sorority Delta Sigma Theta, and many civil rights groups. Her grandmother expected Nikki to pour tea at church programs, to help deliver food to sick people, and even to march in demonstrations. From such activities, Nikki learned the importance of giving to others.

After one meeting at her grandparents' Knoxville church, Louvenia Watson came home bubbling with enthusiasm. A march was to be held to protest a recent hate crime. Grandmother explained that she and Grandpapa Watson were too old to march. She had volunteered Nikki to march in their place. Nikki's grandparents took a cab and met her downtown.

When she was not helping her grandmother, she acted like a typical teenager. She went on double dates to the outdoor drive-in theater. She also read everything from cheap novels to history books.

At Austin High School, Nikki slouched about, looking bored. One teacher, Miss Alfredda Delaney, saw through this behavior and took a special interest in Nikki. A bright, caring, older woman, Miss Delaney was Nikki's English teacher.

Miss Delaney persuaded Nikki to read the works of African-American writers, such as poets Langston Hughes and Gwendolyn Brooks. In 1950, Brooks had been the first African-American poet to win the Pulitzer Prize. Miss Delaney encouraged Nikki to write about what she read. Through these experiences, Nikki became interested in how writers weave words together. At one point, Nikki had planned to become

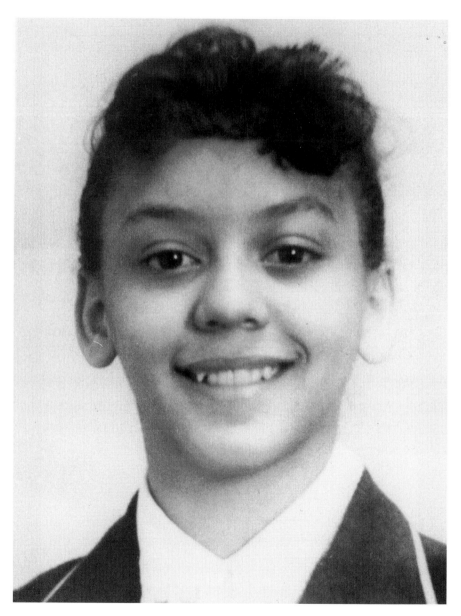

Nikki Giovanni

As a teenager, Nikki read everything from cheap novels to history books.

a lawyer. Miss Delaney suggested Nikki instead consider another path—becoming a writer.

When Nikki was a junior in high school, Miss Delaney and Mrs. Emma Stokes, the French teacher, urged Nikki to apply for early admission to Fisk University. A few days before the admissions test, Nikki and her grandfather took the train to Philadelphia to visit Anto, Nikki's aunt. Grandpapa stayed on with his daughter. Nikki rode the train back to Knoxville by herself to take the exam. Anto had sent Nikki off with a stash of chocolate chip cookies and orders not to talk to strangers.

"At that time, it just wasn't good for a young, black girl to be on a train by herself," explains Giovanni. On the train, some young soldiers stopped and said to Nikki, "She's got chocolate chip cookies and I bet she won't give us one."

Remembering Anto's instructions, Nikki thought a minute, then decided to break Anto's rules. But only a little. Nikki gave each of the soldiers a cookie, but she did not talk with them.[15]

Nikki reached home safely and passed the admissions test. Instead of starting her senior year of high school in the fall of 1960, Nikki, seventeen, entered Fisk University in Nashville, Tennessee. For the first time in her life, she was completely on her own.

4

"DREAMS"

mong Nikki Giovanni's relatives, all children were expected to do three things: clean their rooms on Saturday, attend church on Sunday, and go to college. Grandpapa Watson had graduated from Fisk University in 1905, which was unusual for an African American at that time. In 1960, his granddaughter Nikki enrolled there.

At Fisk, Giovanni jumped feetfirst into a new world of ideas and possibilities. She welcomed the intellectual stimulation. What she did not like were the rules and regulations. Students had to return to the dorm by a certain time, and they could not leave campus without permission. By November, she missed her grandparents. At Thanksgiving break, without permission, she left Fisk and hitched a ride from Nashville to Knoxville.

She had been away just a few months, but her grandfather looked older. Giovanni feared that the end of his life was near.[1] Grandmother Watson was surprised and happy to see Nikki. She did, however, look with disapproval at her granddaughter's chain-smoking and her unfamiliar clothes.

The Monday after Thanksgiving, Fisk's dean of women, Ann Cheatam, called Giovanni into her office. In leaving the campus without permission, Nikki Giovanni had broken a rule. Shaking her head, Dean Cheatam told Nikki that her behavior and attitudes just did not measure up to the ideal Fisk woman. Despite excellent grades, Nikki Giovanni was dismissed from Fisk University as of February 1961.

Nikki's fears about her grandfather's health came true. On a warm spring day that April, John Watson died. Nikki's grandmother had raised and educated three successful daughters and had been an activist and community pillar. Nikki later said, "Yet after we buried Grandpapa . . . it struck me how alone, not only she, but all of us are. . . ."[2]

After Grandpapa Watson's death, Nikki returned to her parents' home in Cincinnati. While Nikki had been away, her sister, Gary, had married and had a son, named Chris. Gary was now divorced.

Giovanni got a job at a Walgreens drugstore as a salesclerk and cashier and enrolled in classes at the University of Cincinnati. In her spare time, she kept a diary and spent time with the children of her mother's social work clients. Nikki read to the children and took them on outings to the zoo, the art museum, and the library.

Like water about to boil, the civil rights movement was steadily heating up across the nation in the early 1960s. Under court orders, schools were trying to bring students of different races together, but conflicts continued. Civil rights activists also wanted to change unjust customs and laws that denied rights to people of color. Some groups preached violence as the only solution to racial inequality. While Nikki Giovanni did not join these groups, she became more and more aware that things needed to change.

One of the leaders that Nikki most admired was Dr. Martin Luther King, Jr. On August 28, 1963, he led the now famous civil rights march in Washington, D.C. A quarter of a million people gathered to hear King deliver his "I Have a Dream" speech. It ended with these words: "And when we allow freedom to ring, . . . we will be able to speed the day when all God's children . . . will be able to join hands and to sing . . . Free at last! Free at last; thank God almighty, we are free at last!"[3]

Two weeks after this speech, Nikki was home alone when terrible news came over the radio. In Birmingham, Alabama, a bomb had exploded in the Sixteenth Street Baptist Church. At the time of the explosion, members of the choir had been putting on their robes in the church basement. The bomb blast killed four young girls and maimed and injured several other people.

Fear swept through Nikki when she heard the news. Remembering her own childhood, she said, "Like all southern youngsters I went to Sunday school in a big church with a basement that could have hidden anything."[4]

Civil rights activists continued to stage marches, carry signs in demonstrations, and challenge public officials. Freedom Riders traveled to the South to assert the legal right of African Americans to sit in *any* seat—not just the back seats—on interstate buses. Sometimes, order broke down and people rioted. White hate groups, like the Ku Klux Klan, responded with increased bombings, beatings, and other violent acts against African Americans.

The Ku Klux Klan had tormented African Americans for years. Looking back at how she felt as a child, Giovanni remembered fear, but also humor. "We used to laugh at the Klan, which liked to think it was the sheets that frightened us. Hell, it was the men in the sheets, and we knew that all along."[5]

Children who marched with their parents sometimes faced police dogs. Many civil rights workers, including Martin Luther King, Jr., spent time in cockroach-infested jails. Of this tension-filled time, Giovanni has said, "You always felt someone was trying to kill you. . . . the summer of 1964 was frightening."[6]

Some positive changes came out of the violence. Dr. Martin Luther King, Jr., won the Nobel Prize for peace in 1964. That same year, the Civil Rights Act was signed into law by President Lyndon Johnson.

In the fall of 1964, Nikki Giovanni returned to Fisk University. There was a new dean, Blanche ("Jackie") McConnell Cowan. Dean Cowan decided that expelling Giovanni from Fisk had been unfair. The dean not only wiped clean Giovanni's past college records but also urged her to continue her studies.

During the next few years at the university, Giovanni majored in history. She edited a student literary journal and reestablished a student group that believed in nonviolent social change.

Her interest in writing grew in 1966, when she worked as an assistant to writer John O. Killens. He was a leader in the Black Arts movement—a group of writers, artists, and musicians who wanted their work to show the rich culture of African Americans.

During the summers, Giovanni visited her grandmother, who had moved to a smaller house on Linden Avenue in Knoxville. The old neighborhood around

400 Mulvaney Street had been torn down to make room for a large housing complex for middle-class white families.

To Nikki Giovanni, her grandmother's new house did not feel like "home." Giovanni wanted to smell hot biscuits, Sunday chicken, and coal ashes. She longed for the gentle sounds of summer breezes, old tunes playing on the radio, and her grandmother saying, "Lord, you children don't care a thing 'bout me after all I done for you."[7]

Giovanni took her grandmother on car trips to Lookout Mountain in Chattanooga, Tennessee. On Sundays, Nikki made ice cream, just as her grandfather always had. By hand, she churned butter. But little by little, she sensed that her grandmother was growing weaker. When they took a walk, Giovanni reached for her grandmother's hand. Both of them knew the truth. The sand in their hourglass of time together was shifting from full to empty. All she wanted, her grandmother said, was to see her favorite grandchild graduate from college.[8]

In December 1966, Louvenia Watson's wish came true. Nikki Giovanni, age twenty-three, graduated with honors from Fisk University with a degree in history. She moved into her own apartment in Cincinnati. Her grandmother had planned to visit on March 10, 1967. But on March 8, Giovanni received a telephone call. Grandmother Watson had died. Nikki's cousin William

Chapman had been with their grandmother at the end.

The day of Grandmother Watson's funeral, Knoxville's Mount Zion Baptist Church was cool and peaceful. Filtered light shone through the windows. People sang her grandmother's favorite hymn, "It Is Well With My Soul," a hymn Nikki loves, too. Nikki Giovanni grieved for "the only person I know for sure whose love I did not have to earn."[9]

The tears flowed freely as Nikki, her mother, sister, Gary, and nephew, Chris, drove back to Cincinnati. Following her grandmother's death, Giovanni threw herself into writing poetry and doing volunteer work. She also edited a local magazine. Her first nationally published article, "First Steps Toward a True Revolution," had appeared in December 1966 in *Negro Digest*. "It made my day," said Giovanni. "There are probably no words to describe the joy you feel when you see your first words in print."[10]

In June 1967, she organized Cincinnati's first Black Arts Festival. The highlight of the festival was a play based on the children's novel *Zeely*, written by Virginia Hamilton. Giovanni wanted young people to know about their African-American roots. From the experience, a black theatrical company formed, called The New Theatre.

Joining the Black Arts movement was Nikki's way of becoming part of the growing Black Power movement,

In the civil rights struggle, Giovanni admired those who preached nonviolence, such as Dr. Martin Luther King, Jr. Her poetry expressed pride in black culture and also reflected the anger of African Americans in a racist white society.

which stressed black pride, dignity, and determination. Because she did not believe in violence, she stopped short of joining forces with more radical black leaders, such as Stokely Carmichael (later known as Kwame Ture), H. Rap Brown, and Malcolm X.

By the fall of 1967, Nikki had made a decision; she would pursue a career in social work. Two important people in Giovanni's life had done social work—her mother and Dean Blanche McConnell Cowen from Fisk. Giovanni began graduate work at the University of Pennsylvania's School of Social Work. A fellowship from the Ford Foundation helped pay her expenses.

As part of her studies, Giovanni worked with groups of teenagers at People's Settlement House in Wilmington, Delaware. After one semester of classes, Giovanni realized that social work was not what she wanted to do. She left the school, but stayed on in Wilmington to work at the settlement house.

On April 4, 1968, a white assassin shot and killed Dr. Martin Luther King, Jr., in Memphis, Tennessee. After hearing the news, Nikki Giovanni jumped into her car and left Wilmington. Within hours, riots broke out there and in many cities all over the country. Giovanni drove through the night to Atlanta, Georgia, to attend King's funeral.

She later wrote these words about Dr. King:

The Funeral of Martin Luther King, Jr.

His headstone said
FREE AT LAST, FREE AT LAST
But death is a slave's freedom
We seek the freedom of free men
And the construction of a world
Where Martin Luther King could have lived
and preached non-violence[11]

Giovanni spent the rest of the spring and summer writing poems. In "Nikki-Rosa," she shared fond memories of her childhood in Ohio. That fall, with a grant from the National Foundation for the Arts, she entered Columbia University's School of Fine Arts in New York City.

Giovanni intended to earn an M.F.A., a master of fine arts degree, in creative writing. A huge boulder blocked the path she had chosen. Professors at Columbia, mostly white, dismissed her work. They told her she could not write.

Nikki Giovanni left Columbia University after only a few months, determined to prove her critics wrong.

5

"REVOLUTIONARY MUSIC"

In 1968, Giovanni had borrowed money from her family and friends to publish her first book of poetry, *Black Feeling, Black Talk*. She delivered the self-published book to stores herself, selling two thousand copies in the first year. She had already published poems and essays in magazines. Yet she had not even tried to find a publisher for her book. She had decided to take her poetry to the people. If they rejected her, that would be that.

Readers did not reject her. They flocked to her poetry readings, drawn to her warm, open personality.

She read her poems in a deep, rich voice, with traces of a southern accent.

Leaders in the Black Arts movement praised her first book. Harsh-sounding racial slurs peppered some of her poems, reflecting the angry climate of the late 1960s and early 1970s. Like other African-American writers then, she wrote mainly for a black audience. Black pride and identity were as important in her work as exposing white racism. Other poems in *Black Feeling, Black Talk* expressed love, playfulness, and appreciation for special people.

In 1969, with the money from sales of *Black Feeling, Black Talk* and a grant from the Harlem Council of the Arts, Giovanni published *Black Judgement*. Again, some poems contained rough-sounding titles and words, such as "Ugly Honkies or The Election Game and How to Win It."

One of the poems, "The Great Pax Whitie," began, "In the beginning was the word / And the word was / Death. . . ."[1] In "For Saundra," she wrote, "maybe i shouldn't write at all / but clean my gun / and check my kerosene supply / perhaps these are not poetic / times / at all."[2]

Reviewers paid the most attention to these revolutionary poems. But other poems were personal—such as "Knoxville, Tennessee," in which Giovanni wrote about feeling warm and safe at her grandmother's home. "For Theresa" honored a family friend who had been kind to Nikki when she was a lonely teenager.[3]

As one reporter described it, Giovanni's words in both her poetry and her speeches ranged from "angry to bitter to sensuous to melancholy to joyful."[4] Most poems had no punctuation or capitalization. This breaking of the rules was typical of many militant writers then.[5] It also reflected Giovanni's view that the flow of words in a poem made punctuation unnecessary.[6]

The year 1969 also marked a personal milestone. Nikki Giovanni became a mother. Thomas Watson Giovanni was born August 31, 1969. Giovanni did not tell people who Thomas's father was. She later explained her decision: "I had a baby at 25 because I wanted to have a baby and I could afford to have a baby. I did not get married because I didn't want to get married and I could afford not to get married."[7]

To support herself and her child, Nikki Giovanni taught writing classes at Queens College in New York and at Rutgers University in New Jersey. In 1970, she formed NikTom, Ltd., a communications company. She also edited and published *Night Comes Softly*, an anthology of poetry by black women.

That same year, Broadside Press published Giovanni's book *Re: Creation*. Its first poem showed that Nikki's life had a new center—her son.

For Tommy

to tommy who:
eats chocolate cookies and lamb chops

climbs stairs and cries when i change
   his diaper
lets me hold him only on his schedule
defined my nature
and gave me a new name (mommy)
which supersedes all others
controls my life
and makes me glad
that he does[8]

Missing from the book were the angry, harsh words of some of her earlier poems. Instead, she brought into sharper focus other important topics: love and the loss of love, the strength of women, self-confidence, and children.

With the birth of her son, Giovanni's life gained a new center—little Thomas. Her new poems began to feature child-friendly topics like napping, mommies, daddies, and rainbows.

In 1971, she made a record called *Truth Is On Its Way*. As she read her poems, the New York Community Choir sang gospel music as background. During the summer of 1971, she introduced the album at a free concert held at Abyssinian Baptist Church in Harlem, New York. A packed audience of fifteen hundred people, including Nikki's mother, listened and applauded.

"It was wonderful," Giovanni said of the people's response. "I was one of the first artists to do a free concert in New York City."[9]

Linking music with her poetry came naturally to Giovanni. Raised on the joyful, stirring music of gospel hymns, she said, "I'm spiritual and I believe that God is black. I was baptized in a Baptist church and my poetry springs partly from this source. What could be more appropriate than having a church for your stage with gospel and poetry together?"[10] *Truth Is On Its Way* stayed at the top of the music charts for weeks.

In 1971 she published a series of autobiographical essays in the book *Gemini: An Extended Autobiographical Statement on My First Twenty-Five Years of Being a Black Poet*. She also published a book of children's poetry, *Spin a Soft Black Song*. The book sparkles with poems about dancing, friendship, napping, mommies and daddies, and scary things in the dark.

Giovanni maintained a demanding schedule—public appearances, teaching, and writing. But every spare minute she had, she spent with her son. Believing that children have to experience life to know it, she wanted Tommy to explore the world around him. When she took him to the zoo, they never went on rides. "We were there to look at the animals and to appreciate the animals," she said.[11]

As Tommy grew, every night he begged his mother for a story.

"I was busy, and sometimes I would say, 'Go read it yourself,'" said Giovanni.

Finally, the little boy said to his mother, "Okay, I will."

"But you don't know how to read," she said.

"Yes, I do," said Tommy, and he read the headlines in *The New York Times* to her. She immediately stopped what she was doing and read him a story.

"I didn't want to punish him for having learned to read, by not reading to him," said Giovanni.[12]

During this time, Giovanni appeared frequently on the public television show *Soul!* Once, she shared the stage with famous blues singer Lena Horne. Horne had fought hard for civil rights. As Giovanni listened to Lena Horne's expressive voice, childhood memories flooded in. Giovanni remembered lying in bed listening to the sound of Lena Horne singing the popular song "Polka Dots and Moonbeams" on television.

Nikki later described the singer's elegance and unique style: "As Lena steps before a camera and walks to the microphone she's got to know she's not alone.

Not only are her ancestors there; mine are too. . . . I still think Lena Horne's untouchable."[13]

In the fall of 1971, Ellis Haizlip, the producer of *Soul!*, asked Nikki Giovanni a question: If she could interview anyone, who would it be?

She did not hesitate. "Jimmy Baldwin. I would go anywhere to talk with him."[14]

Since the early 1950s, James Baldwin had been one of the most famous African-American writers. He had written books, plays, and essays that readers considered daring and controversial. His works included *Go Tell It on the Mountain*, *Notes of a Native Son*, and *Nobody Knows My Name*. Baldwin, tired of living in America where he felt racial oppression, had left the United States. He now lived in France.

Ellis Haizlip arranged for Giovanni and Baldwin to meet in England. By November 1971, she and her son, Thomas, were on a plane to London.

6

"LIKE A RIPPLE ON A POND"

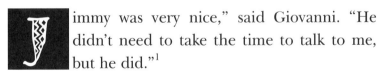

Jimmy was very nice," said Giovanni. "He didn't need to take the time to talk to me, but he did."[1]

In London, James Baldwin often went out at night and did not return to the hotel until dawn. If he ran into Giovanni and her son having breakfast at the hotel, Thomas often shouted, "Jimmy Baldwin! Jimmy Baldwin! Take me for a walk."[2] No matter how tired Baldwin was, he took Tommy for a walk before going to bed.

Nikki Giovanni was twenty-eight, a rising young literary star; James Baldwin was forty-eight, an established

Giovanni was thrilled to interview the famous writer James Baldwin, center. "I would go anywhere to talk with him," she had said. In 1971, television producer Ellis Haizlip, right, arranged a meeting in London, England.

writer and old enough to be her father. For a week, they met and talked in a recording studio. Technicians taped their conversations. Despite the differences in their ages and generations, Giovanni found Baldwin easy to talk to and a good listener.[3]

Baldwin admitted that his generation needed her generation. They discussed what was going on in America—protest marches, sit-ins, boycotts, and demonstrations. He told her that fighting for civil rights was not a new idea:

"Many things which seem . . . new to you are not new to me . . . ," said Baldwin. "A great deal of what passes for black militancy right now is nothing but a fashion."[4]

Giovanni agreed. In many ways, her poetry had moved beyond the hard-line stance taken by many African Americans. Used to thinking for herself and making her own decisions, she had told an interviewer earlier that year: "I believe in a nation built on individualism. If I allow you to be yourself and you allow me to be myself, then we can come together and build a strong union."[5]

In comparing their lives as writers, Baldwin and Giovanni agreed that writers cannot be told what to write. In his writing, Baldwin had drawn upon his own experiences. Nikki Giovanni did too.

Giovanni and Baldwin talked about the importance of giving young people tools to face the future. Giovanni had already observed how easily swayed her college students were. Many wanted to believe in *something*, no matter what. They might just as easily follow a ruthless dictator as a great leader. She wanted to say to such students, "Try believing in yourself."[6]

Giovanni admitted that many black men felt beaten down by white society. Yet she criticized those who acted out their frustration by beating their wives or abandoning them and their children.

"I don't understand how a black man can be nothing in the streets and so fearful in his home," she said, "how he can be brutalized by some white person somewhere and then come home and treat me or Mother the same way that he was being treated."[7]

Baldwin said that many African-American men felt backed into a corner: "How can you explain to a five-year-old kid?—'my boss called me a nigger and I quit.' The kid's belly's empty and you see it and you've got to raise the kid. Your manhood is being slowly destroyed. . . . Your woman's watching it; you're watching her watch it. The love that you have for each other is being destroyed hour by hour and day by day."[8]

Giovanni argued that women of her mother's generation had looked the other way when their men became violent. She said, "My generation says, Hey, no good, you must establish a new base."[9] Despite their differences, she and Baldwin agreed that men and women needed each other.

As the interview drew to a close, Baldwin and Giovanni talked about love, the subject of several of her poems. Giovanni talked about her parents' marriage: "They were able to love each other despite everything."[10]

Baldwin said, "Love is a journey two people have to make with each other."[11]

"I agree," said Giovanni, "and it's awful; we're supposed to be arguing."

"We blew this gig," said Baldwin.[12]

The tape of Baldwin and Giovanni's historic conversation aired in the United States on WNET television in December 1971 on the program *Soul!* and was later published in book form. For Giovanni, sharing the stage with such a well-known writer helped expose her to a wider audience. For Baldwin, establishing a friendship with Giovanni helped him relate to other young African-American writers.

In February 1972, magazine reporter Peter Bailey interviewed Giovanni in New York City. Her apartment was decorated with her own artwork and family pictures. Scattered about were her young son's toys. Bailey asked where the name Giovanni came from. She said, "It just means that *our* [her family's] slavemasters were Italian instead of English or French." Of herself, she said, "I'm black, female, polite, well-educated, and kind to animals and children. I cook well and am kind of short."[13]

On July 25, 1972, Giovanni again combined poetry with gospel music in a poetry recital for more than one thousand people at Lincoln Center. The New York Community Choir accompanied her. One reporter wrote that Giovanni "controlled the reading with her presence and her reading gave the evening its character of . . . joyousness."[14]

Giovanni's new book of poetry, *My House*, also came out in 1972. Rather than talking about anger and revolution, as she had in her first books, many of these poems talked about people reaching out to people through a kind act, a warm smile, and love.

In "Mothers," she recalled her own mother sitting in the kitchen in the moonlight. Yolande Giovanni's long, black hair streamed down her back. She was waiting for Nikki's father to come home from work. *i remember thinking: what a beautiful lady*, Giovanni wrote. In the poem, her mother teaches her the age-old rhyme, *i see the moon / the moon sees me / god bless the moon / and god bless me.*[15]

In "When I Die," Giovanni wrote, *. . . but i do hope someone tells my son his mother liked little old ladies with their blue dresses and hats and gloves that sitting by the window to watch the dawn come up is valid that smiling at an old man and petting a dog don't detract from manhood . . . that touching was and still is and will always be the true revolution.*[16]

Critics of *My House* said that Giovanni had changed. They accused her of "selling out" and "exploiting black people." Critics did not see "touching" and "love" as having anything to do with revolution. One reviewer described Giovanni as a "de-clawed, tamed Panther with bad teeth."[17]

Some of the criticism may have come from the fact that Giovanni was a woman. Most of the leaders of the

Black Power movement were men. Giovanni still felt strongly about many issues affecting African Americans. However, her poetry was moving away from the anger of the 1970s—toward people.

My House established Giovanni as a major new poet. Fans loved the book. Some called her a "poet of the people."[18] On June 14, 1972, she read her poetry on television on the *Tonight Show*, and African-American comedian Flip Wilson interviewed her.

In October 1972, Nikki Giovanni and some other writers were invited to read their work at the Paul Laurence Dunbar Centennial at the University of Dayton in Ohio. Among the other invited speakers was Dr. Margaret Walker, a famous poet, teacher, and writer. Many in the crowded room knew Walker's poem "For My People." People called that poem Walker's "signature poem."

When Walker read her poetry, her eyes twinkled, her lower lip quivered, and her voice rose and fell to emphasize certain words. When she finished, the crowd gave her a standing ovation.

Then it was Giovanni's turn to read. A packed audience buzzed with whispered excitement as the small young woman with the bushy "Afro" hairdo stood before them. She read some of her new love poems in a soft, firm voice, but with a unique "rapping" style. Like Walker, Giovanni received a standing ovation.

Later that day, Giovanni met with Paula Giddings, an editor from Howard University Press. Giddings suggested that Giovanni do a conversation book with Walker. Both poets agreed. The tapings took place over the next three months at Margaret Walker's home in Jackson, Mississippi, and in Paula Giddings's Washington, D.C., apartment. Photographer Jill Krementz captured images of the two poets in conversation.

Like James Baldwin, Margaret Walker, age fifty-seven, came from a different generation of African Americans. She had lived through events and changes that Giovanni had only read about. Lynchings, lack of voting rights, the Harlem Renaissance of the 1920s, and the Great Depression were part of the world in which Walker had grown up. The two writers discussed racial division, unequal opportunities for black and white people, children, discipline, and violence.

At times, Walker and Giovanni interrupted each other. They argued. Editor Paula Giddings chose to stay out of their disputes. Giovanni said, "You mean we're in this fight with no referee? No one is going to ring a bell?" They all laughed.[19]

Despite the differences in their ages and approaches, the women liked each other. Walker said, "I know a lot of people who think you are a brazen hussy. . . . I happen to like you—hussy and all!"[20]

In Giovanni's eyes, Walker was a brilliant writer and human being, smart enough to be a Supreme Court justice.[21]

Walker suggested that an ideal world would be one in which people of many races intermingled. She accused Giovanni of wanting to split the world down the middle between blacks and whites. "I don't want to split the world, it's split already," said Giovanni. "And if that's the way it is, then I want my side to come out number one."[22]

The conversation flowed more smoothly when the women switched to topics they both loved—poetry and literature. They spoke of poets and novelists such as Paul Laurence Dunbar, Langston Hughes, and Richard Wright, as well as more modern writers, such as Gwendolyn Brooks, Leroi Jones (now known as Amiri Baraka), Don Lee, and Ernest Gaines.

Of Giovanni's poem about her childhood, "Nikki-Rosa," Walker said: "I am crazy about that poem. I think it's an absolutely beautiful and wonderful poem. It's a signature poem the way 'For My People' is for me."[23] Walker's words thrilled Giovanni.

By giving of their time, older writers James Baldwin and Margaret Walker created models for Nikki Giovanni to follow. Later in her life, Giovanni said, "Older artists have obligations and responsibilities to younger artists. We have to make ourselves available."[24]

With her popularity growing, Giovanni now found

herself constantly on the road. Her son, Tommy, usually went with her. She traveled to small towns and big cities in the United States, Europe, and Africa, making more than one hundred appearances each year.

"She lectured everywhere, taught anybody who was ready to read and listen," said award-winning author Virginia Hamilton. "She was, indeed, the Princess of Black Poetry."[25]

Giovanni read her poetry to packed audiences of young people, college students, prison inmates, and old people. Crowds clapped and whistled after each poem.

Tommy usually traveled with his mom as she read her poetry to cheering crowds all over the world.

"Her audience starts laughing with her from the beginning," said friend Dr. Daryl Dance of Giovanni's speaking style. "She's honest, direct, and blunt. She shocks the audience with some of her ideas. She takes on everybody. She's tiny but so powerful."[26]

"She's fire and ice," wrote one interviewer. "She generates excitement. Her language is tough and cool. . . . She gives her sermon on success and she talks about love. Sister Nikki is telling it straight; her message is crystal clear."[27]

Hamilton Cloud was a radio disc jockey in New York when Giovanni's album *Like a Ripple on a Pond* came out in 1973. Again, the New York Community Choir accompanied her, under the direction of Benny Diggs.

"People couldn't get enough of it," said Cloud.[28]

Word of Giovanni's work was indeed spreading, like a ripple on a pond.

[Untitled]
(For Margaret Danner)

one ounce of truth benefits
like ripples on a pond
one ounce of truth benefits like a ripple
on a pond
one ounce of truth
benefits like ripples on
a pond
as things change, remember my smile,

the old man said my time is getting near
the old man said my time
is getting near
he looked at his dusty cracked boots to say
sister my time is getting near
and when i'm gone remember i smiled
when i'm gone remember
i smiled
i'm glad my time is getting there

the baby cried wanting some milk
the baby cried needing some milk
the baby he cried for wanting
his mother kissed him gently

when i came they sang a song
when i was born they sang a song
when i was saved they sang a song
remember i smiled when i'm gone
remember i smiled when i'm gone
sing a good song when i'm gone
we ain't got long to stay[29]

7

"Cotton Candy on a Rainy Day"

I n 1973, Nikki Giovanni, age thirty, received a Woman of the Year award from *Ladies' Home Journal* magazine. The other seven women honored at Washington's Kennedy Center included newspaper publisher Katherine Graham, Congress-woman Shirley Chisholm, and actress Helen Hayes.

Some black leaders said Giovanni should not have accepted an award from a mainly white organization. Giovanni disagreed.[1] To her, the award was a sign of progress, something to celebrate. Giovanni accepted the award, and joined the other winners in singing the song "God Bless America."

The award was just one of many of Giovanni's successes that year. *My House* was named one of the best books of 1973 by the American Library Association. Giovanni also published a children's book, *Ego-Tripping and Other Poems for Young People.* The book contained poems about pride, love, loneliness, dreams, rebellion, and patience. In the poem "ego-tripping," she wanted little girls to feel good about themselves and to know about the strength, beauty, and brains of women. Giovanni began the poem:

> *I was born in the congo*
> *I walked to the fertile crescent and built the sphinx*
> *I designed a pyramid so tough that a star*
> *that only glows every one hundred years falls*
> *into the center giving divine perfect light*
> *I am bad . . .*

Boys also liked the sassy confidence of the words in "ego-tripping": *I am a gazelle so swift so swift you can't catch me.* The poem ended with the words: *I mean . . . I . . . can fly like a bird in the sky. . . .* [2] In other poems, "for the masai warriors," and "beautiful black men," she praised boys and men.

In 1974, Giovanni published *A Poetic Equation: Conversations Between Nikki Giovanni and Margaret Walker.* This was followed in 1975 by *The Women and the Men.* The book combined new poems with nineteen previously published ones. She also recorded her poems in studios and released three new albums: *The Way I*

Feel (1975), *The Reason I Like Chocolate* (1976), and *Legacies* (1976).

In 1978, she published a collection of poems called *Cotton Candy on a Rainy Day*. The idea for the title and opening poem had come to her years before when she had taken her young nephew, Chris, on a rainy day trip to the zoo. A concession stand salesperson had refused to sell Giovanni and her nephew cotton candy because the candy might melt. It did not make sense to Giovanni not to eat cotton candy, just because it was raining.[3]

Despite its lighthearted title, *Cotton Candy on a Rainy Day* surprised Giovanni's readers. The subjects of many of the poems were sad and depressing. She wrote about the struggles of African-American women. In "The New Yorkers," she described New York City's homeless people. They live in doorways, cardboard boxes, or underground, like moles, between the subway tunnels and the sewer pipes. In one stanza, an "old blind Black woman" says to Giovanni, *You that Eyetalian poet ain't you? I know yo voice. I seen you on television. . . .*[4]

She dedicated *Cotton Candy on a Rainy Day* to her father, Gus Giovanni. In "Gus," she gave him credit for having worked three jobs to provide for his family. Now an adult herself and a single parent, she better understood her father's frustration when he could not give his children the things they wanted.[5]

Some poems struck a lighter tone. In "The Rose Bush," she remembered childhood days. Nikki, her sister, and cousins would laugh at their grandmother when lightning flashed and Grandmother shouted, *"you children be still   the lightning's / gonna get you."* Giovanni talked about having grown too big to hide beneath the rose bush by her grandmother's porch, the way she once did when playing hide-and-seek with her sister.[6]

In "The Beep Beep Poem," she wrote about driving her car down a lonely country road, feeling the "power in my toe":

> *and i fling my spirit down the highway*
> *i love the way i feel*
> *when i pass the moon and i holler to the stars*
> *i'm coming through*
> > *Beep Beep*[7]

Cotton Candy on a Rainy Day was Nikki Giovanni's twelfth book. By 1978, she had also recorded six albums. For ten years, she had maintained an exhausting schedule of teaching, writing, and speaking.

Then something happened that forced Nikki Giovanni to slow her pace. In 1978, her father, Gus Giovanni, had a stroke. Doctors also said Gus had bladder cancer.

"There was no question," said Nikki Giovanni, age thirty-five. "Mommy needed help. I came home."[8] She left New York City and moved with nine-year-old Thomas to her parents' home in Cincinnati.

The move took her away from New York's publishing world and the writing contacts the city offered.

By 1978, besides teaching and lecturing, Giovanni had published twelve books and recorded six albums.

It also added financial and physical responsibilities to her already full life. But Cincinnati offered a less hectic place to raise a young child. In New York City, she had hired nannies to watch Thomas while she was working. Here she could rely on family members.

Thomas said later that he thought of his grandfather as a kind of "sentry or lazy guard dog." Gus Giovanni would sit in a wicker rocking chair at the kitchen table. Rocking back and forth, smoking a cigar or a cigarette, Gus could see who came to the front door. He would ask visitors questions and gather the news of the neighborhood. Looking out at the backyard, he would let everyone know when the grass needed cutting or the bushes needed trimming.

Thomas studied his grandfather when he "frowned up" at sad news or said "That's so nice to hear!" about good news. Once in a while, Gus Giovanni tried to teach his grandson things, such as where to place a rake so it would not pop up if stepped upon, and hurt someone. As a boy about to become a teenager, Thomas was impressed that his grandfather was not shy about passing gas.[9]

Sometimes when his grandfather was not sitting in the rocking chair, young Thomas climbed up onto it. He settled himself into the big seat cushion and swung his feet back and forth. From this household guardhouse, Thomas imagined that he was keeping watch and making important decisions, just like his grandfather.[10]

"Gus just worshipped the ground he [Thomas] walked on," said Nikki Giovanni. "He would be very upset if Thomas was mad at him. . . ."[11]

Once, when Gus had bushes in the yard trimmed, some birds' nests were destroyed. When Thomas found dead baby birds lying on the ground, he said to his grandfather, "You killed the birds!" To his mother, Thomas said, "I'll help you say grandfather's a fool."

Puzzled, Gus Giovanni turned to his daughter. "Why is the boy mad at me?" he said.

"My father had never apologized to anybody," explained Nikki Giovanni, "So he had to think about it. But finally, he told Thomas he was sorry."[12]

"My father was brave in the face of his impending death," says Nikki Giovanni, "and so was my son. Neither complained of the burden or the pain."[13]

In 1979, Nikki Giovanni published her third children's book, *Vacation Time: Poems for Children*. The book received a Children's Reading Roundtable of Chicago award. Giovanni believes children naturally like the simplicity of poetry. She wants children to read her poems and feel "a sense of whimsy, a sense of wonder, and the ability to look at little things."[14]

"We burden children with explaining the point," Giovanni has said.

"Children should be allowed to respond with their hearts. . . . Poetry is an emotional experience."[15]

"Poetry is an emotional experience," says Giovanni, who encourages children to write their own poetry—from the heart.

The Reason I Like Chocolate

*The reason I like chocolate
is I can lick my fingers
and nobody tells me I'm not polite*

*I especially like scary movies
'cause I can snuggle with mommy
or my big sister and they don't laugh*

*I like to cry sometimes 'cause
everybody says, "What's the matter
don't cry"*

*and I like books
for all those reasons
but mostly 'cause they just make me happy*

*and I really like
to be happy*[16]

8

EVERYTHING IN
PLAIN SIGHT

As her father's health grew worse, Giovanni was needed more and more to help her mother nurse Gus and run the household. She had less time to write and to handle her business affairs.

Nikki's mother, Yolande, asked her friend Gloria Haffer if she would help Nikki with her financial and legal matters. Haffer had worked with Yolande Giovanni in social work, but she had since become a lawyer. Pleased to help, Haffer said yes.

As busy as she was, Nikki Giovanni still visited schools to read her poetry to children. "She went to school after school," said Haffer. "She had very limited time, and yet, she donated her time."[1] Giovanni also helped several of her mother's widowed friends. She did errands for them, took them food, cleaned out their refrigerators, and arranged their closets.

On June 8, 1982, the day after Nikki Giovanni turned thirty-nine, her father died at the age of sixty-seven. Twelve-year-old Thomas went with his mother to the hospital to collect his grandfather's things. Trying to be the man his grandfather had been, Thomas dressed in a coat and tie. Then he helped his grandmother, aunt, and mother pick out a coffin.

Gus Giovanni's death remained painful for his daughter for some time.[2] Rather than return to New York, she and Thomas stayed on in Cincinnati with her mother. The two women had fallen into a comfortable pattern of sharing their living space. They cooked and kept house together. They even had fun remodeling the house together.

In 1983, Giovanni published *Those Who Ride the Night Winds*. Most of this collection of twenty-eight poems had been written using a new form. Giovanni linked groups of words or phrases together with a series of ellipses—three dots—so that each verse looked like a paragraph. These poems were more upbeat than those in *Cotton Candy on a Rainy Day*. She paid tribute to mothers, friends, women, and to important African Americans, like playwright Lorraine Hansberry and civil rights activist Rosa Parks. In 1955, Rosa Parks had refused to give up her bus seat to a white person as required by law in Montgomery, Alabama. After Parks's arrest, Dr. Martin Luther King, Jr., had led a bus boycott. African Americans refused to ride city buses until the Supreme Court forced the city of Montgomery to change the law.

Giovanni continued to look closely at people's lives and at events taking place around her. In some poems, her thoughts tumbled onto the page, like pebbles rushing down a mountain. Other poems, plain and simple, spoke directly to the hearts and minds of her readers.

Like the clear jars in Giovanni's refrigerator, in which colors and textures shimmer and blend, Giovanni likes everything in plain sight, including her poetry: "Most people overlook what they can see. Anything you want hidden, the best place to put it is in plain sight," she said. Talking about her poetry, she says, "I put it out. It's right there. People understand the words, the language."[3] She wants ordinary people to love her poetry. That is why the little things in life— sights, feelings, thoughts, sounds—fall under her writer's microscope.

In "Hands: For Mother's Day," she wrote:

"I think hands must be very important . . . Hands: plait hair . . . knead bread . . . spank bottoms . . . wring in anguish . . . shake the air in exasperation . . . wipe tears, sweat, and pain from faces . . . are at the end of arms which hold . . ."[4]

Giovanni likes everything out in the open, "in plain sight." Like the eggs in Grandmother Watson's egg basket, the little things in life—sights, feelings, thoughts, sounds—fall under her writer's microscope.

In "Charles White," she remembered how good it felt to swing on swings:

Of all the losses of modern life the swing
in the back yard is my special regret
one dreams going back and forth of time and space
stopping bowing to one's sheer magnificence
pumping higher and higher space blurs time
and the world stops spinning while I in my swing
give a curtsey correctly
my pigtails in place and my bangs cut
just right[5]

From 1984 to 1987, Giovanni taught creative writing as a visiting professor of English, first at Ohio State University in Columbus, and then at Mount Saint Joseph's College in Cincinnati. She loved her students and often urged them to read newspapers and magazines and to dig deeper to find answers.

During these years, Thomas was a teenager. His mother wrote, "The fourteen-year-old personality was invented to give ulcers to otherwise calm mothers; to cause normally tranquil, proud, loving parents to snarl, growl and threaten. . . ."[6]

Giovanni had considered enrolling Thomas in a college-preparatory boarding school on the East Coast. Thomas chose instead to stay with his mother and grandmother and attend Cincinnati's Princeton High School.

During high school, Thomas did the usual things teenagers do. He liked to go to parties and did not always work as hard as his mother thought he should. Giovanni insisted that Thomas not lie, ever—even if she said no to his requests. If she did not have a logical reason for denying him something, she told him so, but she stood firm. She would tell him that she understood his anger at her decision.

During this time, Giovanni's travel schedule often kept her on the road. Her mother offered extra help and support. She made sure Thomas was all right.

Giovanni writes poems about people's lives and the events taking place around her. She believes teaching is part of her job as a writer.

"If Mommy said he had to be in by ten o'clock," said Giovanni, "he had to be in by ten o'clock."[7]

Giovanni managed to keep a good mother-son relationship during Thomas's teenage years. She told an interviewer, "I listen to Tommy. I care for him very deeply, but I don't want to be too easy for him. He earns his own money; the way to show love is sometimes to give nothing. He travels with me as often as we can arrange it. If I'm going to any place in the world that he hasn't been, I take him along."[8]

Giovanni's travels also meant that through her poetry readings and her recordings, people recognized her distinctive voice:

"My work offers a singular voice. . . . If you hear my poem you'll know it's me . . . I have as much a signature voice for what I do as Aretha Franklin has a signature voice as a singer."[9]

"All of us like to be read to, whether we're ninety or eight months old," she has said.[10]

Her ability to relate to people remains one of her greatest strengths. "One only has to walk down the street with her—she never turns away from people," said Gloria Haffer. "In Cincinnati, she can't walk a block without being stopped ten times. They say, 'Hi, aren't you Nikki Giovanni?' She is so gracious. People from all walks of life identify with her. That's unusual for a poet."[11]

9

SACRED COWS...
AND OTHER
EDIBLES

In 1987, Nikki Giovanni became a visiting professor at Virginia Polytechnic Institute and State University, known as Virginia Tech. When she left Cincinnati for Virginia, her mother went to live with her older daughter, Gary, in Oakland, California.

Thomas had graduated from high school in June 1987. His mother decided that Thomas should also go to Gary's home in California, where he would be near his older cousin, Chris.

In 1988, Giovanni published a book called *Sacred Cows . . . and other Edibles*. The essays in it covered a wide range of topics—women's rights, the struggles of African Americans, holidays, sports, and commercials. She told readers how much she loves books and also how she works.

Instead of revising parts of a poem, she starts at the top and reworks the whole piece. "A poem's got to be a single stroke, and I make it the best I can because it's going to live. . . . it's at least got to be an accurate picture of what I saw. I want my camera and film to record what my eye and my heart saw."[1]

A friend of Nikki Giovanni's wrote a poem that talked about the power behind Giovanni's carefully chosen words:

For Nikki: Nommo

Nikki, nommo, in the beginning
Took the word and made it into a fist
Which some say, John Henry, still to this day
Tries to open
Which Fannie Lou Hamer had
Bronzed on her nightstand
Which young girls used to wish
Upon a star
Twinkle, twinkle little star
Nikki writes poems that are.

—Margaret B. S. Bristow[2]

Editor's Note: *Nommo* in African folklore means having the power to make things happen by using the right words.

Giovanni believes writers must have passion, deep caring, and sometimes, rage. "Rage is to writers what water is to fish," she said.[3]

Giovanni never asks her readers if they understand her poems. "I just thank them because whether I disappointed or delighted them they took the time to be involved in my effort. . . . It's lonely. Writing. But so is practicing tennis or football runs. So is studying. So is waxing the floor and changing the baby. So is life. We are less lonely when we connect. Art is a connection. I like being a link. I hope the chain will hold."[4]

Giovanni taught at Virginia Tech for two years as a visiting professor. Then she accepted a permanent position in the university's English Department. Popular with the students, Giovanni, in turn, enjoys young people. Teaching gives her the chance to share her life and her work. She also sees teaching as part of her job as a writer.[5] Born into a family of teachers—her grandparents, parents, and aunts—she says, "I bring a high expectation to the profession."[6]

"I want you to travel . . . ," she tells students. "When you graduate and get that plastic money, buy an experience instead of a thing . . . if you buy something and you go broke they can take it from you. . . . Buy yourself a trip or a hundred-dollar meal and it's yours forever."[7]

From her own experiences, Giovanni helps students learn how to take risks as writers and to concentrate.

"I learned [concentration] as a mother," she said.

"After my son was born, there was always noise around. I got used to interruptions. I tell my students with children, 'If you need to study, read what you're studying aloud—the kid is a part of what you're doing.' I have learned that I'm a people person—I enjoy the interaction. I don't need five weeks of silence [to create]."[8]

Always open to talking with her students, she tells them to call her Nikki. "I call them what they call me." If students call her Dr. Giovanni, she puts "Mr.," "Mrs.,"

Giovanni tells her students to travel—to collect experiences, not things. "If you buy something . . . they can take it from you. Buy a trip or a meal and it's yours forever," she says.

or "Ms." in front of their names. "Otherwise you set up inequalities. . . . I respect them; a lot of people in positions of authority don't."[9]

To help students with their writing, she first asks students what they are trying to say. Once they figure that out, she suggests starting with an image, a word picture. Questions such as "Then what?" help the poem take shape. Students read their poetry out loud so they can hear their own words. Above all, she tells them to trust their writing voices and not to be afraid of exposing their feelings.

"You try as a writer to put yourself into the other person's position . . . ," says Giovanni. "Experience is important, but empathy is the key."[10]

"I use poetry as a medium for what I have to say," Giovanni says, "which makes me a poet of information, of content. . . . I like the story and I care more about *what* is being said than *how* it is said."[11]

During these years, Giovanni zigzagged back and forth across the country, sometimes speaking at fifteen or twenty colleges in a month.

"She's one of those rare orators," said Daryl Dance. "She not only reads her poetry, but there's usually a speech or a lecture in addition. I have never seen her speak with notes. The last writer I saw with an eloquence and a personality like hers was Langston Hughes."[12]

"Nikki talks fast, moves quickly," said an interviewer. "Her schedule could be written in quicksilver."[13]

Linking music with her poetry comes naturally to Giovanni, who was raised on the joyful, stirring music of gospel hymns. Here she meets with a gospel choir at Smithfield Plantation in Virginia.

Giovanni believes that two things "choose" you—your car and your profession. One of her cars always started in cold weather. She insists the car said, "Take me!" when she walked onto the dealer's lot. She feels she could have chosen any profession—social work, professional tennis, music. But poetry chose her. The last line of her poem "Boxes" reads, *i write because i have to.*[14]

10

"THE GENIE IN THE JAR"

Ever since she was a little girl, Nikki Giovanni has valued what older people have to say. On clear nights, she used to stand with Grandpapa Watson on his back porch. Gazing at the stars twinkling up above, he told stories about the constellations—Orion's Belt, the Big Dipper, Gemini the Twins. "He always told a good story," she says, "but never the guffaw kind, never the punch line, but always the educational point, always the uplifting parable."[1]

Through the English Department at Virginia Tech, Giovanni taught a writer's workshop at a retirement center called Warm Hearth. Residents there had a lifetime of stories to tell. She encouraged the men and women in her class, many in their seventies, eighties, and nineties, to write stories from their own lives. Little by little, a supportive group of writers formed. Giovanni encouraged her Virginia Tech students to visit the retirement center and learn from the older students. She also brought in famous writers, such as Gloria Naylor and Alex Haley. Soon, relatives of Giovanni's Warm Hearth students began to send them clippings about Nikki Giovanni. It was then that the students realized—their teacher was famous, too.

The Warm Hearth stories and poems became a published book, *Appalachian Elders: A Warm Hearth Sampler*. The book gave these beginning writers great pleasure and pride.

Giovanni followed this with *Grand Mothers: Poems, Reminiscences, and Short Stories About the Keepers of Our Traditions*, published in 1994. Twenty-seven people told stories that highlighted their grandmothers' quirks, nicknames, love, and wisdom. In the foreword to the book, Giovanni wrote: "Grandmothers are special. They talk funny; they think differently; and they are always telling us how much easier we have it." Writing about her own grandmother, Louvenia Watson, Giovanni said, "Grandmother helped me become civilized. She helped me see that little things are all that matter. She taught me patience. She showed me how to create beauty in everything I do."[2]

The last chapter of the book was written by Nikki Giovanni's mother, Yolande, about *her* grandmother, Cornelia Watson. Cornelia Watson was born a free child of slaves. Her parents' owners had taught her to read and write. Called "Mama Dear," this grandmother taught in a one-room schoolhouse for black children. She eventually taught her granddaughters, Yolande and Anna (Nikki's mother and aunt), to read. Mama Dear kept chunks of peppermint in a trunk in her bedroom. If she wanted to reward her grandchildren, she took a cobbler's hammer and chipped off a piece of peppermint. Mama Dear's great-granddaughter, Nikki Giovanni, remembered the peppermint too, even though she was only three or four years old at the time.

Fifty-one when *Grand Mothers* was published, Giovanni was not a grandmother yet. But she has said that she wants to make sure she is ready: "I've been working on my baking because I think all grandmothers should bake. . . . I want my [future] grandchild to say, 'I want to go see Grandma Nik. She always makes great cookies. You've got to prepare for these things. I think it's fun.'"[3]

"As grandmothers, we know what we're doing," she said. "We make quilts, we bake cookies, we say, 'Send that child over here to me.'"[4]

Important family events also took place in 1994. Giovanni's son, Thomas, graduated magna cum laude—with high honors—from Morehouse College in Atlanta,

Georgia. Her sister, Gary, retired and moved with their mother to Virginia to be near Nikki.

That year, Giovanni turned one of her earlier poems into a picture book for children: *Knoxville, Tennessee*. Her words celebrated the strength and power of love.

But in 1995, Giovanni faced an enemy that love couldn't prevent: lung cancer. "I know how sad it is to hear you have cancer," she said. "I couldn't begin to tell you. It's a real bad sound."[5]

As soon as Giovanni learned she had cancer, she told her students at Virginia Tech. With her usual blunt honesty, she said she might not survive the surgery. She warned them that she would not be able to pay much attention to them in the coming months. She gave students the option to drop her class. None of them did. Their loyalty brought tears to her eyes.[6]

Cincinnati surgeons removed the upper lobe of Giovanni's left lung and three ribs. At first, doctors wanted her to stay close to the hospital. Her friend Gloria Haffer, who was away on a family trip, offered to let Nikki stay in her house. Giovanni loved the peaceful setting at the Haffer home: ". . . every day at the kitchen window there were the cardinals eating and doing that little trilling thing they do . . . and I smiled at the birds and felt better. . . ."[7]

After a few weeks, Giovanni returned to the home in Virginia she shares with her colleague and friend,

Ginney Fowler. Each day, Giovanni struggled to get up, shower, and dress. Inside, she felt weak, exhausted, and fearful.[8]

As she rested and tried to get well, a family of robins built a nest in the drainpipe outside her window. She watched as the mother robin turned the eggs daily for two weeks. When the eggs hatched, the robin parents flew back and forth feeding their chirping babies and urging them to fly. During one flying lesson, one of the babies fell to the ground. The baby could not get back to the nest, and it was too big for the mother to carry. Gently, Nikki Giovanni picked up the baby bird and put it in a lined shoe box.

Giovanni cried when she and Ginney finally took the baby robin to a wildlife center. Even if the baby lived, it probably would not return to the mountain. She later

The author of *Grand Mothers* and *Grand Fathers* knows that grandparents are special. Giovanni started practicing her baking and other grandmotherly skills early, just so she'll be ready someday.

wrote a poem called "Me and Mrs. Robin." She said, *I knew she [the mother robin] was seeing her baby for the last time and I thought about how would I feel if I was seeing my son and I hoped she understood that I was just a human being doing the best that I could.*[9]

Some days, Giovanni felt too weak to do anything but watch television. What she saw upset her. "Every other show was a murder. We are making people insensitive; children don't realize what death means. . . . When people die it smells bad . . . fluids come out all over . . . you don't get a bullet in the head and die neatly."[10]

Little by little, Giovanni began to regain her strength. She had quit smoking but missed it enough to dream about smoking. Although she loves food, she was careful to eat and drink in moderation.

"I am a believer in tomorrow; you must believe in spring," Giovanni said. "You want to give yourself every chance to live. If you don't protect yourself, it is going to take you out. You don't fight cancer. . . . Cancer already knows more about you than you know about it." She believes people have to figure out how to live with cancer, how to "dampen it down."

"I'm cheering for me on this one. I'm keeping my fingers crossed."[11]

The Genie in the Jar
(For Nina Simone)

take a note and spin it around spin it around don't
prick your finger
take a note and spin it around
on the Black loom on the Black loom
careful baby
don't prick your finger

take the air and weave the sky
around the Black loom around the Black loom
make the sky sing a Black song sing a blue song
sing my song make the sky sing a Black song
from the Black loom from the Black loom
careful baby
don't prick your finger

take the genie and put her in a jar
put her in a jar
wrap the sky around her
take the genie and put her in a jar
wrap the sky around her
listen to her sing
sing a Black song our Black song
from the Black loom
singing to me
from the Black loom
careful baby
don't prick your finger[12]

Editor's Note: Nina Simone is a well-known jazz singer.

11

"Love in Place"

n 1996, Giovanni published two more books for children. *The Genie in the Jar* danced with images of black songs, black looms, and love. *The Sun Is So Quiet,* a collection of poems, talked about riding rainbows, licking fingers frosted with chocolate, and how to avoid tickling a prickled pickle.

Giovanni's poetry continued to cover a wide range of topics—politics, the environment, current events, and common feelings—mixed with splashes of fantasy, whimsy, and humor.

Giovanni finds nothing humorous about one topic: industrial pollution. Even though her years of smoking

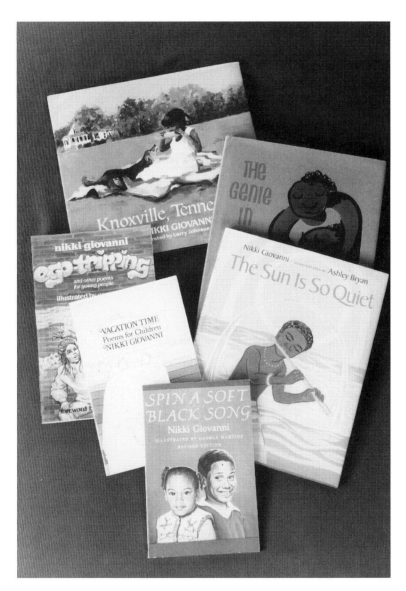

In her poems for children, Giovanni explores themes like friendship, loneliness, dreams, rebellion, and scary things in the dark.

may have caused her lung cancer, she blames polluting industries for other cancers. "I grew up in Cincinnati, which has a very high incidence of cancer."[1]

She is also passionate about protecting animals and the environment. "I don't think it's fair for hunters to take a high-powered repeating rifle to shoot a deer," she has said. She thinks human beings have also killed too many lions, tigers, elephants, cougars, wolves, and panthers.

"Compare your chances of cancer from a polluting industrialist to being eaten by a panther. You'll take the panther any day. The animal has to be injured before it will even look at you."[2]

"Human beings should be better stewards of the earth," she says. "If we want to stay alive, we have to learn to live with other living things." She thinks fences and walls should be built around humans, not animals. "Human beings cannot continue to have unlimited access to the wilderness, because we are afraid. Our response to that fear has been to kill the wilderness. Our response should be to wall ourselves in, because we're the ones who are having the problem.

"In Texas, once a year they go rattlesnake hunting. They don't hunt the rattlesnakes during the time they are even active. You know a rattlesnake doesn't stand a chance against you and a gun. They [the hunters] go into the den. The snake awakes to the sound of shooting. . . .

"Any man that says hunting is difficult has never been to a grocery store. You want something hard?

Find the sauces. Go to Kroger's [a grocery store] and spend all day just tracking down the right kind of peas." Giovanni suggests sending "weekend hunters," armed with paint guns, out onto ten acres of land. Instead of shooting real animals, hunters can shoot decoys. "You shoot and you get the yellow paint on you, and you're officially dead. . . . To hold on to the blood sports as if this is somehow natural is not great."[3]

She tells college students to watch the Weather Channel on television. Then she waits for them to ask, "Why?"

"The winds carry the grains," she says, "and as you study the winds . . . you can see where the breadbaskets are coming from. If you look at it from a Biblical standpoint, Egypt was the breadbasket. That's why everybody had to go to Egypt. In the United States, the Midwest is a great breadbasket and you can see why the winds have brought the seeds, and the rains. You can also see we're losing it. . . . when Mt. St. Helens went up, dust from that volcano ended up in Ohio."

She thinks students can learn from the Weather Channel even when storms *don't* bluster and blow. These calm periods give forecasters the opportunity to explain weather, such as *why* tornadoes, lightning, and thunder happen and *how* people's actions affect the ocean. "We know the fishermen are overfishing, and some of the fish can't breathe. The whales are in trouble. Human beings are in trouble."[4]

Once Giovanni recovered from her cancer surgery, she resumed her fast-paced schedule. In 1996, she published *Selected Poems of Nikki Giovanni*, a collection of poems she wrote from 1968 to 1996. The first poem in the book, "Stardate Number 18628.190," talks about the many contributions of black women, especially mothers. Part of the poem reads:

This is a rocking chair . . . rock me gently in the bosom of Abraham . . . This is a bus seat: No, I'm not going to move today . . . This is a porch . . . where they sat spitting at fireflies . . . telling young Alex the story of The African . . . This is a hook rug . . . to cover a dirt floor . . . this is an iron pot . . . with the left over vegetables . . . making a slow cooking soup . . .

Later in the poem, Giovanni wrote:

It is the faith of our Mothers . . . who plaited our hair . . . put Vaseline on our faces . . . polished our run down shoes . . . patched our dresses . . . wore sweaters so that we could wear coats . . . who welcomed us and our children . . . when we were left alone to rear them . . . who said "Get your education . . . and nobody can put you back"[5]

Meanwhile, Giovanni's son was in law school at Georgetown University in Washington, D.C. Thomas had made his mother proud when he attended the Million Man March held in October 1995. Thousands of African-American men and boys met in the nation's capital for a day of speeches about respecting women, taking care of families, and rejecting violence. Nikki Giovanni considers the march "one of the outstanding events of our century, one that changed how black men looked at themselves."[6]

In 1997, Giovanni published *Love Poems*, a book about the many faces of love. The collection combined some of her earlier poems with twenty new ones. Some poems were funny or downright silly, others passionate or tender:

Love in Place

I really don't remember falling in love all that much
I remember wanting to bake corn bread and boil a ham and I
certainly remember making lemon pie and when I used to smoke I
stopped in the middle of my day to contemplate

I know I must have fallen in love once because I quit biting
my cuticles and my hair is gray and that must indicate
something and I all of a sudden had a deeper appreciation
for Billie Holiday and Billy Strayhorn so if it wasn't love I don't
know what it was

I see the old photographs and I am smiling and I'm sure quite
happy but what I mostly see is me
through your eyes
and I am still young and slim and very much committed to the
love we still have[7]

In "A Poem: for langston hughes," she wrote: *wool is sheared . . . silk is spun / weaving is hard . . . but words are fun.*[8] Early in 1997, Giovanni had received the Langston Hughes Award, given by the City University of New York to honor the great Harlem poet. Previous winners of the award included James Baldwin, Toni Morrison, Ralph W. Ellison, Alice Walker, and Maya Angelou. The director of the festival said, "Like [Langston] Hughes, she has always been a poet of the people."[9]

Giovanni's tattoo, "Thug Life," honors the memory of murdered rap artist Tupac Shakur. "He will be remembered by his people for the great man he could have become," she says.

In 1997, Giovanni won the Langston Hughes Award, named for the great poet. Like him, Giovanni has always been a "poet of the people." Here she socializes at a fish fry in Harlem, New York.

Giovanni dedicated *Love Poems* to Tupac Shakur, a young rap artist. The year before, he had been gunned down in a gang-style killing in Las Vegas. Nikki Giovanni had never met Tupac Shakur, yet she felt he was "cut down before he blossomed."[10] Giovanni called Shakur one "whose name will echo through all the winds whose spirit will flower and who like Emmett Till and Malcolm X will be remembered by his people for the great man he could have become and most especially for the beautiful boy that he was."[11]

Shakur had a tattoo on his chest that read "Thug Life." To honor his memory, Giovanni had the words tattooed on her left forearm.

12

BLUES: FOR ALL
THE CHANGES

ikki Giovanni continues to teach introductory
and advanced creative writing at Virginia
Tech. She also teaches a class about the
Harlem Renaissance, a time in the 1920s when African-
American writers, historians, playwrights, artists, and
musicians drew attention to the culture and experiences
of black Americans.

In Giovanni's Christianburg, Virginia, house,
everything has a place. Eggs rest in Grandmother
Watson's egg basket. Books and records are shelved
in alphabetical order. Giovanni organizes her closet—
by colors, short sleeves, long sleeves, pants, suits.

She even sorts the contents of the shed in her yard regularly.

"I like things in order," she says, explaining what some of her friends call compulsiveness. "I drive my mother crazy."[1]

One room contains objects she calls "Negrobilia," such as sculptures of three black boys eating watermelon and a black man driving a white man in a buggy. The words "Lezzie's Hilltop Hotel for Colored Only" surround a huge blue and green wall clock.[2] Some African Americans collect such objects as a way to remember the past.

Despite her love for order, Nikki Giovanni has her quirks, just as Grandmother Watson did. Giovanni does not keep a personal calendar. "That used to make people uncomfortable," she says, "so now I have one [for appearances]." She also usually relies on others to take care of her financial matters. On trips, she does not read maps well. She prefers to dial 4-1-1 for information instead of looking up something in the phone book.[3]

For many years, Nikki Giovanni wanted to have a community of family and friends around her. In Virginia, she does. Besides Giovanni's mother and sister, her aunt, Anto, lives close by. Ginney Fowler's parents have moved to Virginia, too. "I have always wanted to be a good daughter. I have wanted to make my mother and grandmother proud of me. I like to think I am a good mother; at least I know I did my best," said Giovanni.[4]

She has written about most of her family members. She even dedicated a book—*Spin a Soft Black Song*—to her dog, Wendy, a female cairn terrier, so she would not feel left out.

Giovanni goes out of her way to help others, whether that means writing the foreword to a friend's book or agreeing to give yet another interview. "She's one of the few people I know who take friendship to heart," says longtime friend Linda Dixon. "If she befriends you, she supports you 100 percent. She is very giving and attentive. She's upbeat and positive, and it's infectious. She is one of the kindest people that I know."[5]

Giovanni is still friends with her seventh-grade teacher, Sister Althea. They have kept in touch ever since Nikki attended St. Simon's. "She is the oldest person I have known all my life who isn't a family member," says Giovanni of Sister Althea. "When you're grown, everybody's the same age."[6] Dean Blanche McConnell Cowan of Fisk University was another life-long mentor and friend until her death in 1986.

In her fifties, Giovanni gradually began to allow herself to enjoy life outside of her work. In her spare time, she travels, watches birds, and plays tennis. Television favorites include the Discovery and Learning channels, *Star Trek* episodes, and, always, the

Weather Channel. She also follows baseball, football, boxing, and stock car races.

Sometimes, she sits out on her deck with her dog, Wendy. Over the fence she watches new houses being built. For months, the builders—she calls them "construction monsters"—have been cutting down trees, laying slabs, and hammering boards together.[7] Giovanni worries about the wild animals who have lost their homes. In her yard, birds, squirrels, possums, rabbits, skunks, chipmunks, turtles, groundhogs, and other animals are welcome.

Giovanni thinks animals are highly intelligent. She knows Wendy can tell the difference between a baby bunny and a field rat. Wendy leaves the baby bunnies alone. She kills the field rats because they are mean.

"Before this life is over, I'm going to end up as Beatrix Potter,"

"She supports her friends 100 percent," says Giovanni's longtime friend Linda Dixon, right.

says Giovanni, referring to the English author of the *Tale of Peter Rabbit* and other children's stories.[8]

Like a sponge, Giovanni soaks up details in the world around her. She has always noticed interesting gadgets, rain, clouds, children, feelings. Everywhere Giovanni goes—malls, airports, grocery stores—she studies people and situations. She asks herself, what's the story there? She is working on a book about her cancer experience. A book about aunts will complete her family series.

Nikki Giovanni still cares deeply about people and issues important to her. "Some people soften [as they age]," says editor Doris Cooper. "She hasn't. Nikki is famous for seeing things as they are. She has always been a truth teller."[9]

In the years since the turbulent 1970s, Giovanni thinks progress has been made on civil rights. Yet in the late 1990s, some states ended a policy called affirmative action. This policy had given minorities a greater chance to enter colleges, universities, and other large organizations.

Giovanni sees this backlash against affirmative action as unfortunate. "People clearly need jobs," she says, "but work is not just about money. It's about the dignity of having work."[10] Giovanni has little patience with denying people's rights because of race, gender, or lifestyle. Yet she grows discouraged when African-American students do not take full advantage of the opportunities they have. When students drop in and out of school, she wonders why they don't take their studies more seriously.[11]

"Black Americans are being called to be our best selves," says Giovanni. "Knowledge is power."[12]

She thinks great leaders like Dr. Martin Luther King, Jr., or John F. Kennedy *can* change the way people act. But it is the little people—like Rosa Parks, who refused to give up her bus seat to a white person, or those who marched for civil rights with Dr. King—who *really* make a difference.[13]

Giovanni is on the board of directors for the Underground Railroad Museum and Freedom Center. This national memorial in Cincinnati, opening in 2003, will tell the story of runaway slaves and those who helped them escape to freedom. Louvenia Watson would be proud of her granddaughter.

Colleges and universities still compete to have Nikki Giovanni appear on their campuses. "She has spoken at practically every college in the United States," says Gloria Haffer.[14]

"The students love her," says her friend Linda Dixon, who is assistant dean of students at Miami of Ohio University. "Nikki puts a premium on being able to think for yourself. She tells students, 'You have to question things, read the newspaper, listen to the news . . . think about things.' When she comes on campus, she does not come as a star; she comes as a person. She doesn't hide behind her work, as some speakers do. She talks to the audience; she identifies with them. She's such a bright person and so contemporary—very young at heart."[15]

Nikki Giovanni's playfulness comes through in both her poetry and her personal life. Linda Dixon remembers the first time she and her husband attended a dinner party at Nikki Giovanni's home. Giovanni had grilled huge tiger shrimp and chunks of vegetables. When her guests arrived, she announced that everyone had to eat with their fingers. The reason? The food would taste better. "You couldn't be dainty . . . it was a hoot," said Dixon.[16]

Giovanni's youthful outlook shines through in her comment on her Internet Web site: "If I could come back as anything—I'd be a bird first, but definitely the command key is my second choice."[17]

In 1999, Giovanni published the sequel to *Grand Mothers*, called *Grand Fathers: Reminiscences, Poems, Recipes, and Photos of the Keepers of Our Traditions*. In this book, men and women of all ages, cultures, and races shared memories of their grandfathers.

In the introduction, Giovanni used music to explain: *Grandfathers are notes. Songs that we sing. Not all the songs are happy songs. Not all the songs are good songs. . . . Grandfathers are not uncles or brothers or cousins who can kick the can or play perfect mumblety-peg . . . Open a father and a great grandfather whiffs his way into our lives. . . . it is grandfathers . . . more than any other males, who let us see what loving relationships should be.*[18]

Giovanni wrote about her own grandfather, John Brown Watson. He wove Greek and Latin myths into his stories. On Sundays, he made rich ice cream from eggs, sugar, whipped cream, and vanilla. To him, a meal was not a meal without hot rolls and dessert. Giovanni thinks that some of her more unusual eating habits come from her grandfather. Grandpapa Watson used to toast his bread and then pour cold milk on it, turning the bread to mush. Nikki Giovanni heats her crackers and potato chips, and microwaves her olives.

In a chapter called "Wicker Rocking Chair," Nikki Giovanni's son, Thomas, wrote a moving tribute to his grandfather, Gus Giovanni. Being with his grandfather at the end of his life was a special time for Thomas.[19] He said his grandfather taught him how to be a man. Twenty-eight when he wrote the chapter, Thomas pointed out similarities. Like his grandfather, Thomas mumbles, is strong-willed, and has the ability to absorb information without being easily persuaded. This talent has helped him in his present job as a lawyer. Thomas works for a New York law firm. He married in 1999.

That same year, Nikki Giovanni's book of new poems, called *Blues: For All the Changes*, was published. Giovanni said the poems in it were partly inspired by the late blues singer Alberta Hunter. Hunter once said to Giovanni, "People always talking about the blues, saying it's slow. The blues ain't slow, the blues is truthtelling."[20] The rhythm of Giovanni's book is the blues, but her poems are about change—changes in the world and in Nikki Giovanni's life.

"Betty Shabazz [the widow of Malcolm X] was a change," says Giovanni. "She was murdered. The construction behind my house is a change."[21]

Blues: For All the Changes made the *Los Angeles Times* best-seller list, ranking fourth in the fiction category. It was the first time a book of poetry had ever been listed. In poems both serious and humorous, she wrote about everything from civil rights, the Underground Railroad, and Jackie Robinson, to opening day at the ballpark, rain, singing, and dancing.

On May 18, 1999, New York City celebrated Giovanni's thirty years as a poet. The event took place in Bryant Park, behind the New York City Public Library. Speakers praised her work. Classrooms of children sprawled on the grass, listening and taking notes. Actor and rap artist Queen Latifah read one of Giovanni's poems, "Nothing Is Just." Musicians played.

Music has always been close to Nikki Giovanni's heart. She especially loves jazz—Charles Mingus, John Coltrane, Duke Ellington. She often wears a baseball cap backward that reads "JAZZ." Some of her poems have musical names, as in "Master Charge Blues," "I

Actor and rapper Queen Latifah, right, helps celebrate Nikki Giovanni's thirty years as a poet.

Want to Sing," and "Just Jazz." Book titles such as *Spin a Soft Black Song, Shimmy Shimmy Shimmy Like My Sister Kate,* and *Blues: For All the Changes* have musical roots. She has written poems about African drums, musicians, and dancing:

Three/Quarters Time

Dance with me . . . dance with me . . . we are the song . . . we are the music . . .
Dance with me . . .

Waltz me . . . twirl me . . . do-si-do please . . . peppermint twist me . . . philly
Squeeze

Cha cha cha . . . tango . . . two step too . . .
Cakewalk . . . charleston . . . bougaloo . . .

Dance with me . . . dance with me . . . all night long . . .
We are the music . . . we are the song.[22]

Nikki Giovanni's warmth and honesty have made her one of America's most widely read modern poets, an appeal that crosses age, gender, and race.

"She's 'Nikki' to everybody; she is beloved," said Daryl Dance.[23]

"It's not unusual for Nikki to find three hundred people waiting for her in a bookstore," said Doris Cooper. "She signs books and talks to every one of them. Everybody has a story for her. It's a beautiful thing. At poetry readings, people react as if they've seen an old friend, but also with a mixture of awe and the feeling of being star-struck. Many people know her

"I write because I have to," says Giovanni, whose words capture the energy of the young, the strength of the downtrodden, and the wisdom of the old.

work well. They may pick out a favorite poem. They feel they've come to know *her* through her poetry."[24]

"The most important thing anyone can do . . . is to read," Giovanni has said.[25] She sees poetry as a two-way street: "I share time and thoughts, and the reader shares time and thoughts."[26] Above all, poetry must tell a good story.[27]

For more than thirty years, Nikki Giovanni has invited people to read and to listen to her stories. Performing with the instincts and gifts of an actor, she has read her poetry to the stirring strains of gospel, blues, and jazz, and to the rhythmic tapping of dancing feet.

Nikki Giovanni weaves her magic with words that are simple, honest, wise, and witty. Then she takes the power of her poetry to the people. Again and again, she reminds them:

"We are the music; we are the song."[28]

CHRONOLOGY

1943— Nikki Giovanni is born June 7 in Knoxville, Tennessee; family moves to Cincinnati, Ohio.

1943– Attends Oak Avenue School, St. Simon's in Cincinnati,
–1957 Ohio; visits her Watson grandparents in summers.

1957– Attends Austin High School; lives with grandparents in
–1960 Knoxville, Tennessee.

1960– Begins Fisk University as early entrant but is expelled
–1963 over university regulations in 1961; Grandfather Watson dies.

1964– Returns to Fisk University, and graduates in December
–1966 1966 with a bachelor's degree in history.

1967— Grandmother Watson dies; Giovanni writes poems and begins graduate work at University of Pennsylvania's School of Social Work.

1968— Drops out of graduate school, attends funeral of Martin Luther King, Jr.; moves to New York and briefly attends Columbia University's School of Fine Arts; publishes *Black Feeling, Black Talk*.

1969— Teaches at Queens College and Rutgers University; gives birth to Thomas Watson Giovanni; publishes *Black Judgement*.

1970— Publishes *Re: Creation*; *Black Feeling, Black Talk* and *Black Judgement* are combined and republished as one volume.

1971— Appears on television program *Soul!*; publishes *Spin a Soft Black Song* (for children) and *Gemini*; receives *Mademoiselle* magazine's Highest Achievement Award; releases album *Truth Is On Its Way*; tapes video with writer James Baldwin in London.

1972— Publishes *My House, A Dialogue: James Baldwin and*
–1974 *Nikki Giovanni*, and *A Poetic Equation: Conversations Between Nikki Giovanni and Margaret Walker*; one of eight Women of the Year for *Ladies' Home Journal*; publishes *Ego-Tripping and Other Poems for Young People*; releases album *Like a Ripple on a Pond*.

1975— Publishes *The Women and the Men* and *Cotton Candy on a*
–1978 *Rainy Day*; receives numerous awards and honorary doctorates; releases three albums, *The Way I Feel*, *Legacies*, and *The Reason I Like Chocolate*; moves to Cincinnati to help her mother after her father's stroke.

1979— Is named Cincinnati YWCA Woman of the Year; enters
–1987 Ohio Women's Hall of Fame; publishes *Vacation Time* and *Those Who Ride the Night Winds*; her father dies; honorary commissioner for President Carter's Commission on the International Year of the Child.

1987— Accepts permanent position in English Department at
–1992 Virginia Polytechnic Institute; PBS broadcasts documentary titled *Spirit to Spirit: The Poetry of Nikki Giovanni*; publishes *Sacred Cows . . . and Other Edibles* and *Appalachian Elders: A Warm Hearth Sampler*.

1993— Publishes *Racism 101, Grand Mothers, Grand Fathers*,
–present *Selected Poems of Nikki Giovanni, Shimmy Shimmy Shimmy Like My Sister Kate*, and, for children, *Knoxville, Tennessee, The Genie in the Jar*, and *The Sun Is So Quiet*; receives 1998 NAACP Image Award for *Love Poems*; wins City University of New York's Langston Hughes award; continues teaching, writing, and speaking; publishes *Blues: For All the Changes*; New York City celebrates her thirty years as a poet.

Books by Nikki Giovanni

For Adults

Black Feeling, Black Talk / Black Judgement, 1970

Re: Creation, 1970

*Gemini: An Extended Autobiographical Statement
    on My First Twenty-Five Years of Being a Black Poet*, 1971

My House, 1972

A Dialogue: James Baldwin and Nikki Giovanni, 1973

*A Poetic Equation: Conversations Between Nikki Giovanni
    and Margaret Walker*, 1974

The Women and the Men, 1975

Cotton Candy on a Rainy Day, 1978

Those Who Ride the Night Winds, 1983

Sacred Cows . . . and Other Edibles, 1988

Racism 101, 1994

The Selected Poems of Nikki Giovanni, 1996

Love Poems, 1997

Blues: For All the Changes, 1999

For Children

Spin a Soft Black Song, 1971

Ego-Tripping and Other Poems for Young People, 1973;
    revised 1993

Vacation Time: Poems for Children, 1980

Knoxville, Tennessee, 1994

The Genie in the Jar, 1996

The Sun Is So Quiet, 1996

Edited by Nikki Giovanni:

Night Comes Softly: Anthology of Black Female Voices, 1970
Appalachian Elders: A Warm Hearth Sampler, 1991
*Grand Mothers: Poems, Reminiscences, and Short Stories About
    the Keepers of Our Traditions*, 1994
*Shimmy Shimmy Shimmy Like My Sister Kate: Looking at the
    Harlem Renaissance Through Poems*, 1996
*Grand Fathers: Reminiscences, Poems, Recipes, and Photos of the
    Keepers of Our Traditions*, 1999

Compact Discs and Record Albums

Truth Is on Its Way, 1971, 1993
Like a Ripple on a Pond, 1973, 1993
The Way I Feel, 1975, 1995
Legacies, 1976
The Reason I Like Chocolate, 1976
Cotton Candy on a Rainy Day, 1978
In Philadelphia, 1997

CHAPTER NOTES

Chapter 1. "But Since You Finally Asked"

1. Personal interview with Hamilton Cloud, October 26, 1998.

2. Lorraine Dusky, "Fascinating Woman," *Ingenue*, February 1973, pp. 20–24, 81, 83, reprinted in Virginia Fowler, ed., *Conversations with Nikki Giovanni* (Jackson and London: University Press of Mississippi, 1992), p. 60.

3. Personal interview with Nikki Giovanni, February 17, 1998.

4. Nikki Giovanni, *Selected Poems of Nikki Giovanni* (New York: William Morrow and Company, 1996), p. 287.

Chapter 2. "Nikki-Rosa"

1. Personal interview with Ann Ford, November 17, 1998.

2. Ibid.

3. Personal interview with Nikki Giovanni, November 20, 1997.

4. Nikki Giovanni, *Gemini: An Extended Autobiographical Statement on My First Twenty-Five Years of Being a Black Poet* (New York: Penguin Books, 1971), p. 15.

5. Personal interview with Nikki Giovanni, November 20, 1997.

6. Giovanni, *Gemini*, p 29.

7. Ibid., p. 23.

8. Personal interview with Nikki Giovanni, February 17, 1998.

9. Personal interview with Nikki Giovanni, July 2, 1999.

10. Virginia C. Fowler, *Nikki Giovanni* (New York: Twayne Publishers, 1992), p. 7.

11. Nikki Giovanni, *Sacred Cows . . . and Other Edibles* (New York: William Morrow and Company, 1988), p. 73.

12. Nikki Giovanni, *Black Feeling, Black Talk/Black Judgement* (New York: William Morrow and Company, 1970).

Chapter 3. "Knoxville"

1. Personal interview with Nikki Giovanni, July 2, 1999.

2. Nikki Giovanni, *Gemini: An Extended Autobiographical Statement on My First Twenty-Five Years of Being a Black Poet* (New York: Penguin Books, 1971), p. 6.

3. Personal interview with Nikki Giovanni, November 20, 1997.

4. Personal interview with Nikki Giovanni, February 17, 1998.

5. Personal interview with Ann Ford, November 17, 1998.

6. Giovanni, *Gemini*, p. 10.

7. Personal interview with Ann Ford, November 17, 1998.

8. Nikki Giovanni, *Black Feeling, Black Talk/Black Judgement* (New York: William Morrow and Company, 1970), p. 65.

9. Personal interview with Nikki Giovanni, July 2, 1999.

10. Ibid.

11. Nikki Giovanni, Ed., *Grand Mothers: Poems, Reminiscences, and Short Stories About the Keepers of Our Traditions* (New York: Henry Holt and Company, 1994), Introduction, p. xx.

12. Personal interview with Nikki Giovanni, February 17, 1998.

13. Ibid.

14. Giovanni, *Grand Mothers*, p. xvi.

15. Personal interview with Nikki Giovanni, February 17, 1998.

Chapter 4. "Dreams"

1. Nikki Giovanni, *Gemini: An Extended Autobiographical Statement on My First Twenty-Five Years of Being a Black Poet* (New York: Penguin Books, 1971), p. 7.

2. Nikki Giovanni, ed., *Grand Mothers: Poems, Reminiscences, and Short Stories About the Keepers of Our Traditions* (New York: Henry Holt and Company, 1994), pp. xx–xxi.

3. Martin Luther King, Jr., "I Have a Dream" speech, August 28, 1963, reprinted in E. D. Hirsch, *What Your Sixth Grader Needs to Know* (New York: Doubleday, 1993), p. 34.

4. Nikki Giovanni, *Sacred Cows . . . and Other Edibles* (New York: William Morrow and Company, 1988), p. 49.

5. Ibid., p. 50.

6. Ibid., p. 49.

7. Giovanni, *Gemini*, p. 10.

8. Ibid.

9. Giovanni, *Grand Mothers*, p. xxi.

10. Giovanni, *Sacred Cows*, p. 63.

11. Nikki Giovanni, *Black Feeling, Black Talk/Black Judgement* (New York: William Morrow and Company, 1970), p. 56.

Chapter 5. "Revolutionary Music"

1. Nikki Giovanni, *Black Feeling, Black Talk/Black Judgement* (New York: William Morrow and Company, 1970), p. 60.

2. Ibid., pp. 88–89.

3. Personal interview with Nikki Giovanni, July 2, 1999.

4. Peter Bailey, "I Am Black, Female, Polite . . . ," *Ebony*, February 1972, reprinted in Virginia Fowler, ed., *Conversations With Nikki Giovanni* (Jackson and London: University Press of Mississippi, 1992), p. 32.

5. Personal interview with Daryl Dance, June 24, 1999.

6. Personal interview with Nikki Giovanni, November 20, 1997.

7. Lynn Litterine, "If Revolution Kills Old Women, Then I Don't Want the Revolution," *The Record*, 13 September 1973, reprinted in Fowler, *Conversations*, p. 66.

8. Nikki Giovanni, *Selected Poems of Nikki Giovanni* (New York: William Morrow and Company, 1996), p. 67. Originally published in Nikki Giovanni, *Re: Creation* (New York: Broadside Press, 1970).

9. Personal interview with Nikki Giovanni, July 2, 1999.

10. "Princess of Black Poetry: Nikki Giovanni," *Soul Sounds & Stars*, August 15, 1971, reprinted in Virginia Fowler, *Nikki Giovanni* (New York: Twayne Publishers, 1992), p. 15.

11. Personal interview with Nikki Giovanni, November 20, 1997.

12. Ibid.

13. Nikki Giovanni, *Gemini: An Extended Autobiographical Statement on My First Twenty-Five Years of Being a Black Poet* (New York: Penguin Books, 1971), pp. 87, 89.

14. Personal interview with Nikki Giovanni, November 20, 1997.

Chapter 6. "Like a Ripple on a Pond"

1. Personal interview with Nikki Giovanni, July 2, 1999.

2. Virginia Fowler, *Nikki Giovanni* (New York: Twayne Publishers, 1992), p. 153.

3. Personal interview with Nikki Giovanni, November 20, 1997.

4. James Baldwin and Nikki Giovanni, *A Dialogue: James Baldwin and Nikki Giovanni* (Philadelphia: J. B. Lippincott, 1973), p. 47.

5. Peter Bailey, "I Am Black, Female, Polite . . . ," *Ebony*, February 1972, reprinted in Virginia Fowler, ed., *Conversations With Nikki Giovanni* (Jackson and London: University Press of Mississippi, 1992), p. 37.

6. Baldwin and Giovanni, *A Dialogue*, pp. 61–62.

7. Ibid., p. 43.

8. James Baldwin and Nikki Giovanni, "Excerpt from *A Dialogue*," in Fowler, *Conversations*, p. 71.

9. Baldwin and Giovanni, *A Dialogue*, p. 68.

10. Ibid., p. 68.

11. Ibid., p. 40.

12. Ibid., p. 94.

13. Peter Bailey, "I Am Black, Female, Polite . . . , " *Ebony*, February 1972, reprinted in Fowler, p. 31.

14. Thomas Lask, "Soul Festival: A Cool Nikki Giovanni Reads Poetry," *The New York Times*, July 26, 1972, reprinted in Fowler, p. 60.

15. Nikki Giovanni, *My House* (New York: William Morrow and Company, 1972), p. 7.

16. Ibid., p. 37.

17. Ruth McClain, review of *Re: Creation*, *Black World*, reprinted in Fowler, p. 47.

18. Fowler, *Nikki Giovanni*, p. 60.

19. Nikki Giovanni and Margaret Walker, *A Poetic Equation: Conversations Between Nikki Giovanni and Margaret Walker* (Washington, D.C.: Howard University Press, 1974), p. 39.

20. Ibid., p. 1.

21. Personal interview with Nikki Giovanni, November 17, 1997.

22. Giovanni and Walker, p. 5.

23. Ibid., p. 53.

24. Personal interview with Nikki Giovanni, July 2, 1999.

25. Nikki Giovanni, *Ego-Tripping* (New York: Lawrence Hill Books, 1993, 1993), p. x.

26. Personal interview with Daryl Dance, June 24, 1999.

27. Lorraine Dusky, "Fascinating Woman," *Ingenue*, February 1973, reprinted in Fowler, *Nikki Giovanni*, pp. 55–56.

28. Personal interview with Hamilton Cloud, October 26, 1998.

29. Nikki Giovanni, *My House* (New York: William Morrow and Company, 1972), p. 137.

Chapter 7. "Cotton Candy on a Rainy Day"

1. Virginia Fowler, *Nikki Giovanni* (New York: Twayne Publishers, 1992), p. 16.

2. Nikki Giovanni, *Ego-Tripping and Other Poems for Young People* (New York: Lawrence Hill Books, 1973, 1993), pp. 4–5.

3. Fowler, *Nikki Giovanni*, p. 88.

4. Nikki Giovanni, *Cotton Candy on a Rainy Day* (New York: Morrow Quill Paperbacks, 1980), pp. 29–31.

5. Ibid., pp. 62–65.

6. Ibid., p. 76.

7. Ibid., pp. 68–69.

8. Personal interview with Nikki Giovanni, July 2, 1999.

9. Nikki Giovanni, ed., *Grand Fathers: Reminiscences, Poems, Recipes, and Photos of the Keepers of Our Traditions* (New York: Henry Holt and Company, 1999), pp. 222–223.

10. Ibid.

11. Personal interview with Nikki Giovanni, February 17, 1998.

12. Ibid.

13. Nikki Giovanni, *Sacred Cows . . . and Other Edibles* (New York: William Morrow and Company, 1988), p. 47.

14. Personal interview with Nikki Giovanni, November 20, 1997.

15. Ibid.

16. Nikki Giovanni, *The Sun Is So Quiet* (New York: Henry Holt and Company, 1996), pp. 24–25.

Chapter 8. Everything in Plain Sight

1. Personal interview with Gloria Haffer, May 20, 1999.

2. Barbara Hill Rigney, "A Personal Interview with Nikki Giovanni," *Ohio Journal*, Spring 1986, reprinted in Virginia Fowler, ed., *Conversations with Nikki Giovanni* (Jackson and London: University Press of Mississippi, 1992), p. 160.

3. Personal interview with Nikki Giovanni, February 17, 1998.

4. Nikki Giovanni, *Those Who Ride the Night Winds* (William Morrow and Company, 1983), p. 16.

5. Ibid., p. 28.

6. Nikki Giovanni, *Sacred Cows . . . and Other Edibles* (New York: William Morrow and Company, 1988), p. 45.

7. Personal interview with Nikki Giovanni, July 2, 1999.

8. Rigney, in Fowler, *Conversations*, p. 159.

9. Virginia Fowler, *Nikki Giovanni* (New York: Twayne Publishers, 1992), Appendix: "A Conversation with Nikki Giovanni," October 12, 1991, p. 149.

10. John Mutter, "Authors Blow Kisses to College Booksellers," *Publishers Weekly*, June 3, 1996.

11. Personal interview with Gloria Haffer, May 20, 1999.

Chapter 9. *Sacred Cows . . . and Other Edibles*

1. Claudia Tate, *Black Women Writers at Work* (New York: Continuum Publishing Company, 1983), pp. 73–74.

2. Margaret B. S. Bristow, "For Nikki: Nommo," November 23, 1999, given to the author.

3. Nikki Giovanni, *Sacred Cows . . . and Other Edibles* (New York: William Morrow and Company, 1988), p. 31.

4. Ibid., p. 58.

5. Michael A. Tucker, "The Poet from Lincoln Heights Is No Stranger to Controversy," *Tristate: The Cincinnati Enquirer Magazine*, 20 April 1986, reprinted in Virginia Fowler, ed., *Conversations with Nikki Giovanni* (Jackson and London: University Press of Mississippi, 1992), p. 167.

6. Nikki Giovanni, *Racism 101* (New York: William Morrow and Company, 1994), p. 138.

7. Personal interview with Nikki Giovanni, November 20, 1997.

8. Ibid.

9. Ibid.

10. Fowler, *Conversations*, p. 202.

11. Lois Rosenthal, *Writer's Digest*, February 1989, reprinted in Fowler, *Conversations*, pp. 185–186.

12. Personal interview with Daryl Dance, June 24, 1999.

13. Lorraine Dusky, "Fascinating Woman," *Ingenue*, February 1973, reprinted in Fowler, *Conversations*, p. 53.

14. Nikki Giovanni, *Cotton Candy on a Rainy Day* (New York: Morrow Quill Paperbacks, 1978), p. 34.

Chapter 10. "The Genie in the Jar"

1. Nikki Giovanni, ed., *Grand Fathers: Reminiscences, Poems, Recipes, and Photos of the Keepers of Our Traditions* (New York: Henry Holt and Company, 1999), p. 8.

2. Nikki Giovanni, ed., *Grand Mothers: Poems, Reminiscences, and Short Stories about the Keepers of Our Traditions* (New York: Henry Holt and Company, 1994), pp. xvi–xvii.

3. Tom Smith, "Public Radio Book Show: Nikki Giovanni," WAMC Public Radio, Albany and The New York State Writers Institute, reprinted in Virginia Fowler, ed., *Conversations with Nikki Giovanni* (Jackson and London: University Press of Mississippi, 1992), p. 197.

4. Personal interview with Nikki Giovanni, November 20, 1997.

5. Personal interview with Nikki Giovanni, February 17, 1998.

6. Felicia R. Lee, "Defying Evil, and Mortality," *The New York Times*, August 1, 1996.

7. Nikki Giovanni, *Blues: For All the Changes* (New York: William Morrow and Company, 1999), p. 73.

8. Ibid., p. 74.

9. Ibid., p. 76.

10. Personal interview with Nikki Giovanni, November 20, 1997.

11. Personal interview with Nikki Giovanni, February 17, 1998.

12. Nikki Giovanni, *Selected Poems of Nikki Giovanni* (New York: William Morrow and Company, 1996), p. 84. Originally published in Nikki Giovanni, *Re: Creation* (New York: Broadside Press, 1970).

Chapter 11. "Love in Place"

1. Personal interview with Nikki Giovanni, February 17, 1998.

2. Ibid.

3. Ibid.

4. Ibid.

5. Nikki Giovanni, *Selected Poems of Nikki Giovanni* (New York: William Morrow and Company, 1996), p. 19.

6. Personal interview with Nikki Giovanni, November 20, 1997.

7. Nikki Giovanni, *Love Poems* (New York: William Morrow and Company, 1997), p. 76.

8. Ibid., p. 49.

9. Sally Harris, *Virginia Tech Spectrum*, March 20, 1997.

10. Evelyn White, "The Poet and the Rapper," *Essence*, May 1999, pp. 122–124, 196–198.

11. Giovanni, *Love Poems*, Dedication.

Chapter 12. *Blues: For All the Changes*

1. Personal interview with Nikki Giovanni, February 17, 1998.

2. Felicia R. Lee, "Defying Evil, and Mortality," *The New York Times*, August 1, 1996.

3. Personal interview with Nikki Giovanni, November 20, 1999; personal interview with Gloria Haffer, May 20, 1999.

4. Nikki Giovanni, *Racism 101* (New York: William Morrow and Company, 1994), pp. 134–135.

5. Personal interview with Linda Dixon, June 28, 1999.

6. Personal interview with Nikki Giovanni, July 2, 1999.

7. Nikki Giovanni, *Blues: For All the Changes* (New York: William Morrow and Company, 1999), dedication.

8. Personal interview with Nikki Giovanni, July 2, 1999.

9. Personal interview with Doris Cooper, June 8, 1999.

10. Personal interview with Nikki Giovanni, February 17, 1998.

11. Personal interview with Gloria Haffer, May 20, 1999.

12. Giovanni, *Racism 101*, p. 93.

13. Ibid., pp. 91–92.

14. Personal interview with Gloria Haffer, May 20, 1999.

15. Personal interview with Linda Dixon, June 25, 1999.

16. Ibid.

17. Nikki Giovanni Internet Web site <http://athena. english.vt.edu/Giovanni/Nikki_Giovanni.html> January 5, 2000.

18. Nikki Giovanni, ed., *Grand Fathers: Reminiscences, Poems, Recipes, and Photos of the Keepers of Our Traditions* (New York: Henry Holt and Company, 1999), pp. 3–9.

19. Ibid., pp. 221–228.

20. Evelyn White, "The Poet and the Rapper," *Essence*, May 1999, pp. 122–124, 196–198.

21. Personal interview with Nikki Giovanni, July 2, 1999.

22. Nikki Giovanni, *Those Who Ride the Night Winds* (New York: William Morrow and Company, 1983).

23. Personal interview with Daryl Dance, June 24, 1999.

24. Personal interview with Doris Cooper, June 8, 1999.

25. Laurie A. K. Young, "Nikki Giovanni: Voice of the '60s, Poet of the '90s," *ArtBeat*, July–September 1993.

26. Personal interview with Nikki Giovanni, November 20, 1997.

27. "Nikki Giovanni: First Choice: Poets & Poetry," filmstrip and teaching guide (Pied Piper, 1979).

28. Nikki Giovanni, *Selected Poems of Nikki Giovanni* (New York: William Morrow and Company, 1996), p. 275.

FURTHER READING

Baldwin, James, and Nikki Giovanni. *A Dialogue: James Baldwin and Nikki Giovanni.* Philadelphia: J. B. Lippincott Company, 1973.

Fowler, Virginia C., ed., *Conversations with Nikki Giovanni.* Jackson and London: University Press of Mississippi, 1992.

Fowler, Virginia C. *Nikki Giovanni.* New York: Twayne Publishers, 1992.

Giovanni, Nikki. *A Poetic Equation: Conversations Between Nikki Giovanni and Margaret Walker.* Washington, D.C.: Howard University Press, 1974.

Jago, Carol. *Nikki Giovanni in the Classroom: "The Same Ol' Danger but a Brand New Pleasure."* The NCTE High School Literature Series. Urbana, Ill.: National Council of Teachers of English, 1999.

Strickland, Michael R. *African-American Poets.* Springfield, N.J.: Enslow Publishers, Inc., 1996.

INTERNET ADDRESSES

http://www.math.buffalo.edu/~sww/poetry/giovanni_nikki2.html

http://pages.ivillage.com/crowyne/nikkibio.html

INDEX

Page numbers for photos are in **boldface** type.
Page numbers for complete poems are in *italics*.